Cambridge Elements

Elements in Epistemology
edited by
Stephen Hetherington
University of New South Wales, Sydney

DECEPTION AND SELF-DECEPTION

A Unified Account

Vladimir Krstić
United Arab Emirates University

Shaftesbury Road, Cambridge CB2 8EA, United Kingdom

One Liberty Plaza, 20th Floor, New York, NY 10006, USA

477 Williamstown Road, Port Melbourne, VIC 3207, Australia

314–321, 3rd Floor, Plot 3, Splendor Forum, Jasola District Centre, New Delhi – 110025, India

103 Penang Road, #05–06/07, Visioncrest Commercial, Singapore 238467

Cambridge University Press is part of Cambridge University Press & Assessment, a department of the University of Cambridge.

We share the University's mission to contribute to society through the pursuit of education, learning and research at the highest international levels of excellence.

www.cambridge.org
Information on this title: www.cambridge.org/9781009509770
DOI: 10.1017/9781009362887

© Vladimir Krstić 2025

This publication is in copyright. Subject to statutory exception and to the provisions of relevant collective licensing agreements, no reproduction of any part may take place without the written permission of Cambridge University Press & Assessment.

When citing this work, please include a reference to the DOI 10.1017/9781009362887

First published 2025

A catalogue record for this publication is available from the British Library

ISBN 978-1-009-50977-0 Hardback
ISBN 978-1-009-36289-4 Paperback
ISSN 2398-0567 (online)
ISSN 2514-3832 (print)

Cambridge University Press & Assessment has no responsibility for the persistence or accuracy of URLs for external or third-party internet websites referred to in this publication and does not guarantee that any content on such websites is, or will remain, accurate or appropriate.

For EU product safety concerns, contact us at Calle de José Abascal, 56, 1°, 28003 Madrid, Spain, or email eugpsr@cambridge.org

Deception and Self-Deception

A Unified Account

Elements in Epistemology

DOI: 10.1017/9781009362887
First published online: July 2025

Vladimir Krstić
United Arab Emirates University
Author for correspondence: Vladimir Krstić, drpop1@yahoo.com

Abstract: Received theories of self-deception are problematic. The traditional view, according to which self-deceivers intend to deceive themselves, generates paradoxes: you cannot deceive yourself intentionally because you know your own plans and intentions. Non-traditional views argue that self-deceivers act intentionally but deceive themselves unintentionally or that self-deception is not intentional at all. The non-traditional approaches do not generate paradoxes, but they entail that people can deceive themselves by accident or by mistake, which is controversial. The author in this Element argues that a functional analysis of deception solves these problems. On the functional view, a certain thing is deceptive if and only if its function is to mislead; hence, while (self-)deception may but need not be intended, it is never accidental or a mistake. Also, self-deceivers need not benefit from deception and they need not end up with epistemically unjustified beliefs; rather, they must 'not be themselves'. Finally, self-deception need not be adaptive.

This Element also has a video abstract:
www.cambridge.org/EEPI_Krstic_abstract

Keywords: deception, self-deception, misleading, intention, function

© Vladimir Krstić 2025

ISBNs: 9781009509770 (HB), 9781009362894 (PB), 9781009362887 (OC)
ISSNs: 2398-0567 (online), 2514-3832 (print)

Contents

Preface	1
1 Introduction	1
2 Human Deception	8
3 A Functional Analysis of Self-Deception	23
4 The Not-So-Beneficial Result of Self-Deception	43
5 Concluding Remarks	59
References	61

Preface

This *Element* is a product of eleven years of work, but it does not contain the idea that I initially intended to defend. I initially thought that we should understand deception as a kind of manipulation and then model self-deception on this, manipulativist, conception of deception. This is how I thought the famous 'paradoxes of self-deception' should be resolved. However, arguments put forward by Don Falls in his 'What Is Disinformation?' and Marc Artiga and Cédric Paternotte in their 'Deception: A Functional Account' made me change my mind. I now argue that the best way to understand deception and self-deception is to apply a functional description to the phenomena: we have deception (or self-deception) when the function of the thing that misleads is to mislead. I think that this not only gives us an easy way out of the paradoxes of self-deception but also allows us to explain all kinds of deception (human and biological) using one simple and effective theory.

The claim that the view I defend here is capable of explaining all cases of deception (including self-deception) is rather ambitious, and one may naturally wonder whether it is possible to do something so ambitious in such short space. After all, this is an *Element* and, as such, it is constrained by a strict word limit. True, this word limit prevents me from discussing certain views or developing certain sub-arguments in more detail. However, I do not find this to be a debilitating flaw in the argument: it does not prevent me from presenting the main argument in sufficient detail. In fact, I think that this strict word limit is an *Element's* virtue. I do not want the reader to read long literature reviews or spend time pondering about some issues that, while important for some reasons, are not central to the phenomena in question. I want their attention to be focused on the gist of the problem: the most important problems in our analyses of self-deception are caused by our incorrect accounts of interpersonal deception, and we can solve these problems elegantly by defining deception in functional terms. *Elements* is a perfect venue for publishing a rather clear, concise, and focused argument in support of a promising general analysis of self-deception.

> This argument is an investment in the future. I am hoping that my account will serve as a firm basis for future analyses of the two phenomena, and my future arguments will certainly offer further refinements and details.

1 Introduction

In this Element, I offer an analysis designed to capture all instances of deception and self-deception, both human and biological, and – believe it or not – I do this by modelling self-deception on interpersonal deception. But how do I manage to achieve one such ambitious feat?

My key move is to define interpersonal deception in functional terms rather than by appealing to the deceiver's intention and, then, model self-deception on this analysis. On the view I defend, we have deception if and only if the function of the thing that misleads is to mislead. This move allows us to easily model self-deception on interpersonal deception without generating the dreaded 'paradoxes of self-deception'. An additional upside of the view is that it defines deception in self-deception not only in the same way it defines deception in interpersonal deception but also just as it defines deception in biological deception. Put simply, it delivers a unified account of deception: biological deception, human deception, and self-deception are all captured by the same simple view. And when I say 'self-deception', I mean both human and (possible) animal self-deception: for if an organism can engage in deception and be a victim of deception, it can engage in self-deception as well; hence, those organisms that can deceive and be deceived can also be self-deceived. In what follows, I will first explain why we need a functional analysis of self-deception, since this phenomenon is more difficult to understand, and then outline my view in detail. I then proceed to my argument.

According to the so-called *traditional* approach, self-deception is modelled on interpersonal deception. On this view, that is, people deceive themselves intentionally just as they deceive others intentionally. Both the process and the outcome of self-deception are intentional: the person φ-s intentionally (e.g., directs her attention away from some evidence) to cause herself to believe that *p* in a situation in which she already believes that not-*p* or thinks that this is what she should believe. Typically, the distress associated with the thought that not-*p*, or the thought that they ought rationally to believe it, motivates self-deceivers to cause themselves to believe that *p* (Davidson, 1986: 208; see, Gur and Sackeim, 1979).

Unfortunately, this description requires that self-deceivers intentionally make themselves believe as true what they already believe is false and that they hide from themselves their deceptive intention, and this seems impossible. Specifically, self-deceivers should, at some point, not only consciously and simultaneously believe both that not-*p* (as deceivers) and that *p* (as victims) but also cause themselves to believe that *p because* they believe that *p* is false. And although some successful theories of the mind explain how people simultaneously hold contradictory beliefs (Egan, 2008; Quilty-Dunn and Mandelbaum, 2018; Bendaña and Mandelbaum, 2021), none can explain situations in which one belief causes the other in this way. This is the so-called *Doxastic* or *Static paradox* of self-deception (Mele, 1987: 138). Another problem comes from the fact that deceivers must hide their deceptive strategy from their victim (if you know that I am lying, you will not believe my lie). This causes the so-called *Strategy* or *Dynamic paradox* of self-deception (Mele, 1987: 138): self-deceivers should, simultaneously, both be aware of their deceptive strategy (as deceivers) and not be aware of it (as victims), and a unified and reasonably coherent mind cannot simultaneously both be and not be aware of the same thing; this violates the law of non-contradiction.

For these reasons, many traditionalists (e.g., Davidson, 1986, 1997; Pears, 1982, 1986, 1991; Lockie, 2003; Mijović-Prelec and Prelec, 2010; Curzer, 2024a, 2024b; see Deweese-Boyd, 2021; Funkhouser, 2019: §4) posit that the self-deceiver's mind is fragmented in a sense that allows that one agent-like, semi-autonomous part of the mind could mislead another part or the agent as the 'main system'. This solution, however, does not solve the paradoxes in the way traditionalists need them to be solved: *the self* needs to deceive *itself* (the same agent) and, on this hypothesis, one agent deceives another agent. Another serious problem is that this kind of mind-fragmentation is very severe (Johnston, 1988): these agent-like parts seem to be too autonomous and often difficult to define. Finally, this hypothesis is unfalsifiable (it cannot be proved wrong), which is a very serious flaw that the literature does not address. Other traditionalists try to resolve the paradoxes by appealing to conscious *versus* unconscious processes in our minds (Pataki, 1997; Lockie, 2003; Funkhouser and Barrett, 2016; Funkhouser and Hallam, 2024; against, Doody, 2017). However, while this division is less severe and easier to understand, the hypothesis is still unfalsifiable (see, Derksen, 2001) and the self fails to genuinely deceive itself.

Sorensen (1984) and Bermúdez (2000) posit logically distinct subjects and suggest that, in self-deception, one temporal stage of a person deceives another temporally distant stage – by hiding some information, for example. However, while the self here indeed deceives itself, this is its-future-self, and we want to understand *real-time* self-deception (Davidson, 1986: 208; Johnston, 1988: 76–78; Scott-Kakures, 1996: 41–42; Levy, 2004: 298). In Krstić (2023a; see 2020a, 2024a), I offer an analysis of lying by asserting a proposition one believes to be true but judges (without believing) to be false and argue that this person can deceive her-current-self by lying; she could intend to make her inaccurate credence even less accurate (see, Krstić, 2023b). While this argument avoids the concerns that apply to the mind-partitioning and the temporal partitioning views and explains why some self-deceivers exhibit tension or seem to know the truth deep down, it captures only one (rather rare) kind of self-deception.

Because of these serious problems, many scholars think that self-deceivers do not need to intend to mislead themselves. Consider this case.

> *Maria* possesses much evidence that her husband, Arnold, a famous actor and bodybuilder, is having an affair. Arnold is a real character. He spends most of his time exercising, he loves any kind of positive attention, especially from

the ladies, and he likes to enjoy a good Cuban cigar. None of this *per se* is a particularly concerning problem: Maria knows that Arnold enjoys life and perhaps loves himself a bit more than he should. The problem is that Arnold has lost sexual interest in Maria, he has protected his phone with a password, and she sometimes picks up what appear to be subtle love signals he exchanges with one of his female co-actors. Yet, despite having access to all this evidence, Maria retains her belief that Arnold is not having an affair, a belief that seems so evidently false to all her friends and relatives.

Maria is not being wilfully ignorant, she does not appear to be trying (i.e., intending) to deceive herself, and she does not selectively focus only on favourable evidence. Rather, she retains her belief by what looks like explaining away the pieces of information that cause her distress without realising that she is thereby keeping herself misled. When her girlfriends voice their concerns to her, she says that Arnold protected his phone with a password because he leaves it on the set while shooting his scenes and that his sexual desire decreased because he has stopped taking his protein shakes (which increase it). 'Exchanging subtle love signals merely reveals flirting, not an affair' – Maria keeps insisting – 'Many people flirt without having any further intentions. Arnie is just trying to keep the on-screen chemistry with his colleague'.

Maria is a milder version of Mele's (2001: 26) – now dated – case of Sid.

Sid is very fond of Roz, a college classmate with whom he often studies. Wanting it to be true that Roz loves him, he interprets her refusing to date him and her reminding him that she has a steady boyfriend as an effort on her part to 'play hard to get' in order to encourage Sid to continue to pursue her and prove that his love for her approximates hers for him. As Sid interprets Roz's behaviour, not only does it fail to count against the hypothesis that she loves him, it is evidence *for* the truth of that hypothesis.

Even though they did not intend to deceive themselves, Maria and Sid are self-deceivers according to the so-called *deflationary* approach. Mele (1987, 1997, 2001, 2010, 2020), Barnes (1997), Holton (2001), Nelkin (2002), Levy (2004), Funkhouser (2005, 2009), Van Leeuwen (2007a), Scott-Kakures (2009, 2021), Galeotti (2012, 2018), Lauria, Preissmann, and Clément (2016), Lynch (2012, 2017), and Wehofsits (2023) are some proponents of this view. Some deflationists allow that a desire can directly (and pre-consciously) distort belief formation without any intermediary intentional action (Lazar, 1999; Mele, 2001; Lauria, Preissmann, and Clément, 2016), and some see this as a full description of self-deception (Johnston, 1988; Fingarette, 1998). These subtleties and differences matter but not for my argument. What matters is that these solutions do not generate the two paradoxes because they 'deflate' the intention to deceive: their central thesis is that self-deceivers act (sub-)intentionally but deceive themselves unintentionally and unknowingly. However, this idea entails that deception can occur accidentally or by mistake – causing epistemic harm is an unforeseen by-product of the person's behaviour – and misleading by accident or by mistake does not count as deception (§2.1).

Finally, according to some views belonging to what I call *revisionist* solutions, self-deception is when the self ends up with a false belief, typically about itself (Lazar, 1999; Patten, 2003; Fernández, 2013). This generates the same problem as deflationism: the agents have simply made a mistake (e.g., they make a faulty inference about what they believe). Other revisionists posit that self-deceivers end up with some novel, often hybrid, mental states (Audi, 1982; Lazar, 1999; Egan, 2009; Jordan, 2019, 2020). And some suggest that self-deceivers engage in a kind of pretence (Gendler, 2007; Korczyk, 2024) or that they avoid exercising some (unpleasant) thoughts (Bach, 1981, 2009; Marcus, 2019). These solutions entail that self-deceivers are deceived in a figurative sense of the word, and they often misclassify mere errors and accidental misleading as self-deception. Thus, they also divorce self-deception from deception.[1]

So, all three families fall short of a satisfactory analysis of self-deception. I argue that the solution to all problems is simple. Animals and plants need not mislead intentionally but they nonetheless do not mislead by accident or mistake: misleading is the function of their behaviour. Human behaviour can also be captured in functional terms: the description under which a person intends to φ gives us the function of φ-ing, and non-intentional human behaviour also has a function. Therefore, I argue that (self-)deception can be unintentional when the function of the behaviour or the trait whereby the self misleads itself is to mislead. In my view, that is, we have self-deception when a person acts in a specific way (exhibits a specific trait), the function of that behaviour (trait) is to mislead, and it causally contributes towards her ending up misled.

There is much to be gained and nothing to be lost from adopting this approach. Adaptations (traits evolved by natural selection) have a purpose in the same way intentional behaviours do (Artiga and Paternotte, 2018: 581). Therefore, shifting to a functional analysis of human deception significantly improves our grasp of human deception (by capturing both intentional and non-intentional behaviour) and keeps the distinction between deceiving and simply misleading; it provides a more sophisticated analysis of interpersonal deception at no cost. More importantly, a functional analysis of self-deception will neither necessarily generate

---

[1] I call accounts 'revisionist' if they revise some important concepts: for example, if they posit that the product of self-deception is non-doxastic or that it is a hybrid between a desire and a belief, or that self-deception is a mere error. Deweese-Boyd (2021) classifies deflationist theories as 'revisionist', but I disagree: they do not revise but rather offer a rival account of human deception. Notice, my brief review focuses only on a few revisionist theses (see, Deweese-Boyd, 2021; Funkhouser, 2019: §5).

paradoxes, since intending to deceive is not necessary for self-deception, nor will it count mere mistakes or accidental self-misleading as self-deception, since the function of the thing whereby the self misleads itself is to mislead. Finally, while I claim that intending to self-deceive is not a conceptual requirement, the view easily captures cases of intentional self-deception: If I intend to deceive myself by lying, then misleading is the function of my lie.

With the correct theory of deception in place, then, modelling self-deception on interpersonal deception need not be paradoxical. And since self-deceivers genuinely end up epistemically worse off on this analysis, there is no need to appeal to novel mental states in an ad hoc manner or to count mere pretence or avoiding a thought as deception. Finally, even though the view does not deny the existence of cases involving intentional self-deception, it entails that these are not the 'classic' cases of self-deception. The classic cases have a functional description and are easy to understand (§3).

Another important advantage of this model, call it *the functional view*, is that it captures (a) all cases of human deception and self-deception, (b) all cases of biological deception, and even (c) cases of possible animal self-deception; it can capture *all* deception. For example, Angilletta, Kubitz, and Wilson (2019) argue that the behaviour of some weak crayfish involves self-deception (also, Šekrst, 2022: 10–13): crayfish that have large claws but little muscle beneath may escalate aggression as if they are ignorant of their real strength (it is not in their interest to escalate aggression). This ignorance and engaging in a very dangerous behaviour (they risk serious injury) explain why one might infer that weak crayfish are self-deceived. We do have pre-theoretical reasons to see this as a case of self-deception. Crayfish can engage in deception (big claws but small muscles), and they can be victims of deception. Therefore, it is conceptually possible that they can engage in self-deception as well.

Because pretty much all analyses of self-deception appeal to higher-order mental states (excluding Johnston, 1988; Fingarette, 1998; Livingstone Smith, 2014), they must hold that lower-level animal self-deception is impossible, or that it is a different kind of self-deception (Barnes, 1997; Scott-Kakures, 2002). In contrast, because the function of having large claws when your muscles are small is to mislead, the functional view can classify this trait as self-deceptive without the need to posit higher-order mental states in crayfish, and it does this by modelling self-deception on other-deception.

The functional view does not force us to think that this is animal self-deception, but it does give us clear conceptual grounds to support our position (whatever it may be). The advantage of the view is that, if this is animal self-deception, it will clearly tell us why *and* this explanation will be supported by a hypothesis that applies to *all* kinds of deception; and, if this is not self-deception, the view will tell us why by appealing to *the same* universally applicable hypothesis. For instance, one may object that this is not self-deception because deception is not directed at the self. This objection applies only if deception must be directed at someone, and below I argue that it need not. However, one could argue that weak crayfish are bluffing, and you cannot be deceived if you did not suffer any epistemic harm, and thus, this is not self-deception.

Because it models self-deception on interpersonal deception, my view could be considered as the traditional view refined. And because it assumes that intending to deceive is not necessary for deception, it could be understood as refining the deflationary view. I prefer to understand it as a novel approach to deception and self-deception: the whole point of my argument is that it resolves serious issues in existing accounts of self-deception before they arise, namely, by refining our analysis of interpersonal deception. And I am offering a detailed analysis of all deception. No received view does that. Nevertheless, I do not think that the view loses its appeal if we classify it as belonging to either of the two families. The most important thing is that it solves our most pressing problems.

This Element has five sections. §2 offers an analysis of human interpersonal deception. In §2.1, I contest the view that self-deception can include misleading by accident or by mistake. In §2.2, I put forward a functional account of human deception. §2.2.1 presents my functional analysis of human deception, §2.2.2 discusses some examples of non-paradigmatic human deception, and §2.2.3 resolves some objections.

§3 features a functional analysis of self-deception. In §3.1, I apply my functional analysis of human deception to self-deception and argue that we have self-deception when a person behaves in a certain way or exhibits a specific trait, the function of this behaviour or trait is to mislead, and she thereby misleads herself. This analysis does not generate paradoxes, since the intention to (self-)deceive is not necessary for self-deception, and it does not misclassify misleading by mistake or accident as deceiving, since the function of the behaviour/trait is to mislead. In §3.2, I argue that self-deception is a motivated internal irrationality, and that the most reliable method of identifying self-deception is seeing whether the person deviates from her normal behaviour, whether she is 'not being herself'. In §3.3, I apply my theory to *Maria* and *Sid*.

In §4, I analyse various theories as to why organisms engage in self-deception. I argue that, just like any kind of deception, self-deception is not necessarily adaptive and that some kinds of self-deception may actually be maladaptive. The best solution, then, is a case-by-case analysis of self-deception. §5 briefly concludes my argument.

2 Human Deception

2.1 The Intentionalist and Deflationary Analyses

A satisfactory analysis of deception must provide a non-arbitrary criterion to rule out cases where someone was misled accidentally or by mistake (Skyrms, 2010: 76; Fallis, 2015b: 383; McWhirter, 2016: 759; Artiga and Paternotte, 2018: §2; Fallis and Lewis, 2019: 2282). This is why the predominant ('intentionalist') view requires that human deception is intentional (Linsky, 1963; van Horne, 1981; Barnes, 1997; Mahon, 2007, 2016; Carson, 2010; Faulkner, 2013; Saul, 2013). We know that I did not mislead you by accident or mistake because I intended to mislead you. Such a view implies that, when it comes to human behaviour, deceiving someone and unintentionally misleading them are two distinct phenomena.

The foundation of deflationism is the idea that, while self-deceivers acted intentionally, they did not intend to deceive themselves; the action was intentional under some other description. Therefore, what deflationism counts as self-deceiving is unintentional self-misleading according to the intentionalist analysis of human deception. Notice, when applied to self-deception, the intentionalist analysis does not entail that one can deceive oneself into believing that p only if p is guaranteed to be false. Rather, it entails that if the self-deceiver's belief is false, what explains this fact is that they intended to cause themself to believe *a falsehood* or *an unjustified* belief, not just a specific belief.

Alfred Mele, however, famously rejects this view. He writes: 'Yesterday, mistakenly believing that my son's keys were on my desk, I told him they were there. In so doing, I caused him to believe a falsehood. I deceived him ... ; but I did not do so intentionally, nor did I cause him to believe something I disbelieved' (Mele, 1997: 92). Mele thinks that (1) one can intentionally or unintentionally cause someone to believe what is false and that (2) one can cause someone to acquire the false belief that p even though one does not believe that not-p. I wholeheartedly agree with both claims, but I also think that his argument fails (Krstić, 2024c: 837) and that the example is incorrect. It is not a mistake or an accident that Mele's son believes the keys are on his desk: Mele wants him to believe this. However, it is a mistake that the son believes a *falsehood*: Mele intends to inform him. Thus, because misleading by mistake is not deception, Mele does not deceive but rather mislead his son unintentionally.

We may rightly refer to Mele's behaviour in everyday conversation with the word 'deceive', but this is irrelevant to our discussion. People often use words like 'deceive' or 'lie' in some broader senses that cannot prove a philosophical point. When I say 'Your smile is a lie', I am not using the term 'lie' in the sense in which we understand lying to oneself; here, 'lie' means 'fake'. And when statistics lie, they create a false or misleading impression. Similarly, if I cause you to believe falsely that *p* by mistake, you may say 'You deceived me', but I will respond 'Yes, but it was a mistake'. I could also say 'I did not mean to. My memory deceived me'. This is a coherent communicative exchange, but 'deceive' is used in the meaning of '(merely) mislead'. When I say that my memory or my eyes deceived me, I am personifying the process that generates my false belief by describing it as if it were the action of another agent who has tricked me into believing what I believe. Because many different senses of a term are often conflated in general use, we cannot rely on just any coherent or meaningful use of 'deceive' or 'lie' if we want to understand self-deception or establish a conceptual truth. Rather, we need to engage in conceptual analysis, which is why I am offering an account of self-deception grounded in a conceptual analysis of deception.

But it could be that there is an additional element that makes unintentional *self*-misleading count as deceiving even though unintentional *interpersonal* misleading does not. Mele (1987: 123) seems to distinguish unintentional interpersonal deception from unintentional self-deception. He and other deflationists assume that, in self-deception, the coming to believe against the weight of available evidence is not accidental or random because acquiring or maintaining the belief is appropriately motivated (Mele, 1987). One case in point is Mele's reply to Audi.

Audi (1997: 104) invites us to imagine that, wanting to believe that *p* is true, I discuss the matter only with people who believe this, and I thereby expose myself to one-sided evidence for it. At one instance, I speak to Eva, who believes that *p*, and she convinces me that *p* is true. Audi thinks that I have now non-deviantly acquired a false belief by treating relevant data in a motivationally biased way (i.e., Mele's conditions for entering self-deception are satisfied) but that this is not self-deception. Eva may have convinced me by using a good argument for a plausible hypothesis that happens to be false. The idea seems to be that I have, as a result of a desire, acquired a false belief by happenstance and that the deflationary view gives a false positive here.

However, in response, Mele (1997: 131) argues that my coming to believe that *p is* deviant: I met Eva by accident. Even though I am biased, my desire did not cause that I meet someone capable of convincing me that the proposition that I want to believe is true. Thus, we do not have a false positive here. Here is how deflationism eliminates misleading by accident. Deflationists presume that certain desires and interests, when powerful enough and in the right circumstances, have predictable effects on our reasoning (e.g., Mele's famous 'for ways of self-deception'), and these desires and interests typically have little to no intimate relationship to the truth. Therefore, because the causal relationship between biasing and belief acquisition is non-deviant, if there are *ceteris paribus* laws describing the effects of desire and interest on reasoning e.g., the FTL hypothesis testing, see §3.1), this secures the non-accidentality requirement.

We see that, on the deflationary view, the relevant interest or desire non-accidentally generates the false belief in self-deception. However, accidental misleading and misleading by mistake are not synonyms (Austin, 1956). When something is accidental, it is a coincidence, it is caused by some external factor. It happened by chance, like meeting Eva. A mistake, however, is when you do something wrong. It is an action/event that departs from the purpose a thing is designed to achieve by existing as it exists or acting as it acts. And you do not meet Eva by mistake. Meeting her was not your fault. It was a random event.

Austin's example might explain the difference better. Say that you and I both have a donkey, which graze in the same field. One day, I decide to shoot mine. I aim, fire, and the animal falls. But when I come closer, I see I killed your donkey. I killed your donkey by mistake. Say now that I decide to shoot mine but that – as I fire – my donkey moves and I hit yours. Killing your donkey was an accident (Austin, 1956: 11, n. 4). This translates into our discussion in the following way. Suppose that I mistakenly believe that Sydney is the capital of Australia. If I tell you that Sydney is the capital of Australia, I mislead you; I do not deceive you. If you come to me upset about this false belief, I will tell you that I had misled you by mistake. However, if I want to text you a smiley face but I trip and press a sad face, I mislead you by accident. An external factor is responsible for your false belief that I am sad.[2]

Mele misled his son about the whereabouts of the keys by mistake but not by accident: this was the exact belief Mele intended to cause in his son, and causing it did not involve a deviant causal chain. However, the belief was not supposed to be false; Mele made a mistake, he gave his son the wrong piece of information. The same applies to the deflationary analysis of self-deception. The self-deceiver does not mislead himself by accident, but he does mislead himself by mistake: he wants his belief to be true. While not reasoning based on your evidence increases the probability of making a mistake, and while we may be able to predict the outcome of the behaviour, this is still a mistake. And this is the fundamental problem with the deflationary analysis of human deception and self-deception. Even if intending to mislead is not necessary for deception, misleading by mistake cannot count as deceiving. Notice, I am not arguing that cases of motivationally biased reasoning – that is, cases like *Sid* – are not cases

---

[2] Austin (1956: 28) also distinguishes mistakes from errors; he writes that, 'in an *accident* something befalls: by *mistake* you take the wrong one: in *error* you stray'. If I believe that Canberra is the capital of Australia but I misspeak and tell you 'Cranberra', I mislead you by error. For the sake of simplicity, I will treat mistake and error as synonymous.

of self-deception. I argue that the causal role of desires and interests is, by itself, insufficient for self-deception and that, thus, deflationism fails to capture deception in these cases; it captures only the 'entry' condition for self-deception.

In response, it has been suggested to me that deflationism is wrong only if self-deception needs to be a particular instance of deception. And because deflationists do not model self-deception on deception, they can accept that self-deception is not deception. Whether we call this 'deception' or not is ultimately irrelevant, this person thinks, 'the important question is whether deflationism can account for the phenomenon illustrated by cases such as Sid's'. First, I am not sure that deflationists do not model self-deception on deception; rather, they argue that interpersonal deception need not be intentional. Second, to simply say that self-deception is not deception is to beg the question. The burden of proof is not on me to show that self-deception is a species of deception. The burden of proof is on the objector to show that it is not. Third, the fact that deflationism can account for the phenomenon illustrated by cases such as Sid's cannot establish the theory's plausibility. The theory of phlogiston could account for combustion perfectly well, but it was misguided. In addition to having sufficient explanatory power, a theory needs to be internally and externally consistent, and deflationism lacks external consistency in a significant way.

Traditionalists should not gloat here. The same applies to their partitioning the mind solution: even if this hypothesis explains the phenomenon, this is not evidence that it is correct. Therefore, the facts that it is unfalsifiable, rather radical, and that we have better candidates (see, e.g., Borgoni, Kindermann, and Onofri, 2021) are strong reasons against it (see, §3.3). A successful falsifiable theory of self-deception consistent with analyses of both intentional and biological deception that does not need to posit new entities should surely be preferred over theories that lack these qualities. Staunch deflationists have to say that human interpersonal deception is one kind of deception, that human self-deception is a different kind of deception, and that animal self-deception is the third kind of deception. A functional analysis can successfully explain these three phenomena using only one account of deception that is consistent with our most basic assumptions about human and biological deception. Staunch traditionalists will have to abandon the idea that self-deception is modelled on interpersonal deception and say that self-deception is a kind of interpersonal deception. A functional analysis can easily model self-deception on interpersonal deception.

More importantly, the deflationary view can easily be functional. Deflationists are correct (1) that deceivers need not intend to deceive and (2) that they need not believe the opposite of what they intend to cause in their victim. The problem is not the thought that people can deceive unintentionally and unknowingly but rather the theory's inability to eliminate misleading by mistake. And this is exactly what traditionalists are trying to avoid. Therefore, we just need a theory that will not misclassify misleading by mistake or accident as deception, and I am offering one. Both deflationists and traditionalists can benefit from this view.

I now proceed to present my functional analysis of human paradigmatic (intentional) and non-paradigmatic (unintentional) deception.

2.2 A Functional Analysis of Human Deception

2.2.1 The Theory

Theories of biological deception appeal to selection pressure, payoffs, or functions of behaviours, traits, or states (of the world) rather than the deceiver's intentions. The most common philosophical analyses of biological deception are signalling-based and, on the predominant ('Skyrmsian') view, a signal S is deceptive iff (1) S is false, (2) transmitting S systematically benefits the sender, and (3) the receiver is misled or suffers harm from responding to the signal (e.g., Searcy and Nowicki, 2005; Skyrms, 2010; McWhirter, 2016; Shea et al., 2018; Fallis and Lewis, 2019, 2021). Because the sender systematically benefits from sending this false signal, there is a mechanism (e.g., selection pressure) that reinforces the sending of such a signal (Fallis and Lewis, 2019: 2283). Thus, it is not an accident or a mistake that the receiver is misled or harmed.

According to one rival signalling-based analysis (Birch, 2019), deception requires that, by sending a deceptive signal, a sender strategically exploits an adaptive disposition in a receiver by raising the probability, from the receiver's standpoint, of a non-actual state of the world. Therefore, we have deception iff (1) signal S changes subjective probabilities of states in the wrong direction, (2) sending S is a part of the sender's strategy that exploits a particular adaptive disposition in the receiver to perform behaviour B in the non-actual state of the world whose subjective probability the signal raises, and (3) the receiver is misled by S. A strategy is any pattern of behaviour that can be transmitted by an inheritance system down the generations and characterised with conditionals of the form 'If in context C, perform behaviour φ / activate trait Φ' (Birch, 2019: 31). The fact that the exploitation is strategic (involves a transmittable pattern of behaviour) *and* that the strategy targets particular dispositions in the sender eliminates situations in which the signal is false by accident or mistake (Birch, 2019: 31). The sender need not benefit from this.

Finally, according to Artiga and Paternotte's (2018) 'functional' analysis, a state of the world M is deceptive iff (1) M has the (etiological) function of causing a misinformative state (or to prevent the acquisition of new information) and (2) M leads to a misinformative state. In presenting this view, I will refer to functions of behaviours (e.g., playing dead) or traits (e.g., teeth-like colouration on one's skin) of organisms rather than states to make the argument easier to follow. The fact that the function of M is to mislead eliminates situations in which misleading was an accident or a mistake. The deceiver need not benefit from this. Also, since some strategies of deception do not seem to involve signalling (Artiga and Paternotte, 2018, 2024; Krstić, 2025), the functional view has a broader scope than the signalling-based analyses.[3]

Because it sits comfortably with the existence of altruistic deception (Artiga and Paternotte, 2018; Birch, 2019) and non-adaptive self-deception (§5), and because it is not limited to deception involving signalling (Artiga and Paternotte, 2018, 2024; Krstić, 2025), I proposed (Krstić, 2024c) an analysis of human deception developed along the lines of Fallis's (2015a) functional analysis of disinformation and Artiga and Paternotte's (2018) functional account of deception. Let us first present the theory on a simple example of biological deception and then cash it out as a general theory of human deception.

Western hog-nosed snakes deter predators by simulating death. This is deception on my version of the functional view because

(1) 'Deterring predators' (F) is the (beneficial) *result* of 'the snake's simulating death' (M) in context C ('predators present'),
(2) In C, simulating death (M) generates this result (F) by misleading,
(3) Misleading is the *function* of simulating death in C, and
(4) The snake's simulating death (M) misleads the predators.

The variables are F (a specific result), M (a specific behaviour/trait), and C (the relevant context). The idea is that because the function of M in C is to mislead and M generates F in C by misleading, M systematically generates F in C. When cashed out as conceptual analysis, we get that, for a specific behaviour/trait M, result F, and context C, we have deception when

(1) F is the *result* of M in C,
(2) F is generated by misleading in C,
(3) The *function* of M in C is to mislead, and
(4) (In part) because of (3), M causally contributes to misleading.

Six important clarifications need to be made. First, I use 'mislead' in the meaning of 'move further away from the truth' or 'cause a false representational state' (Artiga and Paternotte, 2024). On this terminology, a misleading

---

[3] Krstić (2025) offers a more detailed comparison of these views.

signal is a signal that carries misinformation, a false signal ('misleading' refers to its content), not a signal designed to mislead. A signal whose function is to mislead is deceptive. Also, some believe that a deceptive signal is always false. Fallis (2015a), for example, defines disinformation as misleading information that has the function of misleading. However, on my view, some deceivers may use true signals to cause epistemic harm (Krstić, 2025, 2024b: §3, §4); thus, a deceptive signal need not be misleading (i.e., false). To avoid confusion, I will refer to a misleading signal as a 'false signal' or 'misinformation'. Relatedly, I cannot define what counts as ending up misled or epistemically worse off in all situations – since what counts as epistemic harm is notoriously difficult to define – but this should not be seen as a debilitating flaw. My goal is not to provide a definition of misinformation. I just need concepts that may help me explain the nature of deception, and we do have a sufficiently good grasp of the relevant concepts.

Second, my analysis provides a minimal condition for deception, which is that the function of the thing that misleads is to mislead. This is consistent with the existence of intentional deception. If I φ intending to thereby deceive, then my intention gives us the function of my φ-ing. Say that I intend to trick you into wiring me $10 ('for the transfer fee') by telling you that your distant uncle from Nigeria left you a fortune. I lie to you intending to get your money, but I intend to get your money *by* causing you to believe a falsehood. Causing you to believe this falsehood is in the description under which my lie is intentional. I intend *both* to deceive you and to get your money.

Third, I understand 'function' and 'result' as defined by Garson's (2019) *generalised selected effects* theory (GSE). According to GSE, in short, a proper function of something is whatever it was recently selected for by natural selection or some comparable selection process. Proper functions are *proximal* functions. The remainder is beneficial consequences or more distal selected effects of the thing performing its function; the remainder is the *result*. The function of the heart is to beat, not to circulate blood. The circulation of the blood is a beneficial result of the heart's performing its function (Garson, 2019: §7; Fagerberg and Garson, 2024; against, Artiga, Schulte, and Fresco, forthcoming). Analogously, when I lie to you about the supposed uncle from Nigeria, the *function* of my lie is to cause you to believe that you have a dead uncle in Nigeria. Getting your money is the beneficial *result* of you believing my lie, and (as said) I intend both the result and the function (to deceive).

On this theoretical framework, just as the circulation of the blood is the beneficial result of the heart's performing its function (to beat), the deterring of the predators is the beneficial result of the snake's simulating death performing its function (to mislead). Typically, the result explains why a specific trait or behaviour has this specific function in this specific context. The snake's simulating death has a systematic tendency to deter predators (produce a certain effect) in the relevant context precisely because its function is to mislead, which explains why the snake engages in deception rather than in honest communication; revealing the truth will not generate this effect. However, misleading need not be directed at some specific target. Even though the snake engages in deception to deter predators (i.e., *this result* explains why it plays dead), it may also mislead non-predators. Misleading non-predators also counts as deception (the function of the behaviour is to mislead) even though this result does not explain why the snake plays dead.

Fourth, the distinction between 'result' and 'function' is crucial. Normally, the reason for deceiving is the deceiver's practical benefit (the 'result') and misleading is the means of achieving this end: the deceiver gets what he 'wants' by misleading the dupe. *The result*, thus, *explains why an organism engages in deception* in this context, while *the function explains why this is deception*. Causing you to acquire the false belief that your distant uncle from Nigeria has left you a fortune is a means by which I get your money, and it explains why I intend to deceive you. However, my getting your money (the result) does not constitute deception – since you may give me the money knowing that I am trying to con you. Rather, it is causing you to believe my lie (the function) that constitutes deception, and if this happens, we have deception even if you do not give me the money.

My fifth important point is that satisfying conditions 3 and 4 (function) constitutes deception; these conditions are necessary and jointly sufficient for deception. Conditions 1 and 2 (result) are there to provide further information relevant to the ensuing analysis of interpersonal non-paradigmatic deception and self-deception. With more relevant similarities between examples of non-paradigmatic human deception and uncontroversial cases of biological deception, my argument will be stronger. This is why I will compare exemplary cases of biological deception with some cases of human behaviour and, based on the analogies, argue that human behaviour may involve deception even when the deceivers do not intend to mislead.

Finally, this terminology has a threefold purpose regarding the relevant analysis of self-deception. First, it easily captures both intentional and non-intentional deception. Second, it makes it clear that achieving some practical result (i.e., alleviating anxiety, increasing one's happiness) by misleading the self is *not* a sign of self-deception – since misleading could have been an accident or a mistake. Thus, the terminology should keep us focused on what is essential for self-deception. Third, establishing this focus allows us to classify the relevant cases correctly. The terminology, that is, guides our inquiry in more productive ways.

Let us apply this functional analysis to an exemplary case of biological deception. This case will serve as a benchmark against which I will compare analogous cases of human deception, including self-deception.

> *Fireflies* use their light for sexual signalling. While flying over meadows, male fireflies flash a species-specific signal. For instance, the Photinus firefly produces a yellow-green flash. If a female Photinus on the ground gives the proper sort of answering flashes, the male descends and they mate. An exception to this practice is the behaviour of female fireflies of the genus Photuris. When one of these fireflies observes the flash of a male of the genus Photinus, she may mimic the Photinus female signals and, if she does this, it is to lure the male Photinus in and eat him.

The yellow-green flash is standardly understood as meaning something like 'I am a Photinus female ready to mate' or as raising the probability of the state in which this female is present (Skyrms, 2010; Birch, 2014, 2019; Shea et al., 2018; Skyrms and Barrett, 2019; Fallis and Lewis, 2021). Therefore, the signal is false when sent by the predator Photuris female, and because it is false and sending it both systematically benefits the sender and is a part of a strategy that exploits the receiver's adaptive disposition to descend to mate, the signalling-based analyses classify this as deception. This is deception in my view as well:

(1) The predator female transmits the yellow-green flash because the food tends to come down to her when she sends it,
(2) The signal generates this result (bringing her food) by misleading,
(3) Misleading is the behaviour's function in this context, and
(4) Because males descend to mate rather than to get eaten, they count as being misled.

However, and this is vital for the correct understanding of human non-paradigmatic deception, the predator female does not send this signal because she 'wants' to mislead. Her behaviour is an evolutionary adaptation (a product of simple trial and error) caused by the fact that misleading rather than informing harmless males in this context causes them to descend. Simply put, the predator female sends this signal because the food tends to come down to her when she sends it. Her food comes down because her food-calling flash is their mating flash, but she does not know that. She *only has the beneficial result 'in mind'* and this result fully explains why she sends this specific signal in this specific context (i.e., when she 'wants' to eat) and why the signal means 'I am a Photinus female ready to mate' rather than something else (e.g., 'I am blue').

Paradigmatically, people know exactly what they are doing when they engage in deception, but I think that many cases of interpersonal deception are analogous to *Fireflies*: some people engage in a certain behaviour and *are aware of their behaviour's result but not of its function*. This is why I understand human deception and self-deception in functional terms. The predator 'knows' that the food tends to come down when she sends the signal, but she does not 'know' that the food comes down because the signal misleads it. Analogously, because they are unaware of their behaviour's (trait's) function, non-paradigmatic human deceivers do not intend to mislead even when they intend the result. The behaviour's function is an adaptation (cultural, evolutionary, etc.) caused by the fact that a specific kind of dishonesty systematically generates the required response on the part of the victims. Intentional deception is caused by the same fact; the only difference is that intentional deceivers also intend the means whereby they generate this response.

This might seem complicated, but it is actually very simple. To show what I mean, I proceed to compare cases of non-paradigmatic human deception with *Fireflies* (§2.2.2); the analogies between them are striking. I will then consider an objection to my analysis (§2.2.3) and proceed to develop the relevant functional analysis of self-deception (§3).

2.2.2 Non-Paradigmatic Human Deception

Recall, my view easily applies to intentional deception. When I tell you that your distant dead uncle from Nigeria has left you a fortune and that I need $10 for processing fees, I intend to get your money by causing you to believe my lie. Since proper functions are proximal functions, the function of my lie is to mislead, and it is a part of the description under which my behaviour is intentional. Getting your money is the lie's beneficial result, just as the circulation of blood is the beneficial result of the heart's beating.

Let us now apply the view to non-intentional interpersonal deception. Consider an interesting piece of advice for APA interviews (Krstić, 2021, 2024c). The advice is *Don't 'be yourself'* (Arvan, 2015). Rather than being yourself, you should create

> a professional persona . . . [namely,] a full-fledged adult who demonstrates a tightly organized research program, a calm confidence in a research contribution to a field or discipline, . . . innovative but concise, non-emotional ideas about teaching at all levels of the curriculum, . . . and . . . a steely-eyed grasp of the real . . . needs of actual hiring departments. (Kelsky, 2012)

People who have just finished their PhD can hardly have a steely-eyed grasp of the real needs of actual hiring departments, they are rarely confident in their teaching and research, and they often apply for jobs for which they are not a perfect fit. For these job seekers, the advice 'don't be yourself' genuinely means 'present yourself as *a different person*, the perfect candidate'. This advice is sensible, but this is also exactly what one predator female firefly would say to another. Just as a job candidate does not want to transmit a message that means 'I am not the best candidate, but I need you to give me this job', the predator firefly does not 'want' to transmit a signal that means 'I eat harmless males and I need you to come down'. The 'not being themselves' job candidates pretend to be the perfect candidate by mimicking the behaviour of the perfect candidate in the same way the predator female firefly pretends to be a sexually receptive female by mimicking her signal.

In most cases, job candidates do not realise that they are acting deceptively by not being themselves, and, thus, they do not intend to deceive. And even though they only intend to get the job by not being themselves, that is, they intend the behaviour's *result*, misleading is nonetheless the function of their behaviour: the members of the search committee should think that they are the perfect candidate. An extremely high selection pressure explains the function of this behaviour: because only 3.5 per cent PhDs manage to secure a position in academia (Taylor et al., 2010: 14), candidates have the best chances of getting a job by presenting themselves as being perfect for the job. Therefore, when this behaviour misleads, this is not an accident or a mistake. Not being oneself in this context is deception because

(1) Getting the job is the beneficial *result* (F) of this behaviour (M) in this context (C),
(2) This result is generated by misleading,
(3) The *function* of the behaviour in C is to mislead, and
(4) The behaviour misleads.

One reason to think that this is not deception is that conditions 3 and 4 are not satisfied: everyone understands that this is a formal interview and that a candidate's behaviour is a performance, like being on stage. One could say that, if the members of the search committee are impressed by the candidate and think that they are clearly hireable, that would count as a success of the candidate's performance – since they are trying to make a good impression in the interview. And because everyone sees this as performance, the function of the behaviour is not to mislead, and it does not mislead. I think differently. We cannot compare academic job interviews with performances of this kind. The candidate's performance must be an indicator of actual qualities: Havier Bardem did not get an Oscar for his role in 'No Country for Old Men' because the committee thought that he would be a great psychopathic killer. Moreover, unlike performances of figure skaters or gymnasts, the 'not being themselves' candidates mimic qualities they do *not* have. Therefore, even if everyone really thinks that this is a formal interview and that a job candidate is 'performing', unlike a figure skater but just like an actor, a candidate can purposefully mislead by mimicking qualities that they do not have. For instance, they could misrepresent themself as having exceptional tolerance or patience.

Let us now consider a case that involves using the poisonous 'belladonna' (*Atropa belladonna*) plant to make one's pupils dilate and acquire a dusky, lustrous appearance of one's eyes. Because this appearance was the height of beauty in Renaissance Italy, Venetian ladies used belladonna extract to dilate their pupils and make themselves look more beautiful (Passos and Mironidou-Tzouveleki, 2016: 766; Carlini and Maia, 2017: 66). Dilated pupils make people look more beautiful for a very important reason: people's pupils dilate the most when they are looking at someone they find sexually stimulating. Men and homosexual women are most attracted by large pupils in women, while heterosexual women are most attracted by medium-sized pupils in men (Tombs and Silverman, 2004; Rieger and Savin-Williams, 2012) and, correspondingly, women's pupils dilate more than men's (Lick, Cortland, and Johnson, 2016). Arguably, this discrepancy in preferences exists because males and homosexual females are most attracted to large pupils because their reproductive strategies are best served if they can avoid missing a mating opportunity with an interested partner (Tombs and Silverman, 2004; Lick, Cortland, and Johnson, 2016). Heterosexual females are predisposed to favour more moderate sexual attentions to avoid possible physical harm.

When we put this together, we gain two important insights: First, the *false* impression that a woman with large pupils is sexually aroused makes her appear more attractive; people think that the woman looks more attractive *because* they are misled by the size of her pupils. Second, generating this false impression is the function of dilating pupils. The parallel with *Fireflies* is clear: the woman sends a false signal about her sexual receptiveness by dilating her pupils just as the predator female firefly sends a false signal about her identity and sexual receptiveness by sending a yellow-green flash. Therefore, using belladonna to send a false signal in Renaissance Venice involves deception for the same reasons the predator female firefly's sending the false signal involves deception. On my analysis, using belladonna involves deception because:

(1) The *result* of dilating pupils (M) in this context (C) is to look more attractive (F).
(2) This result is in C generated by misleading: a woman looks more attractive because she gives the false impression that she is sexually aroused.
(3) The *function* of dilating pupils in C is to mislead (cause this false impression).
(4) Dilating pupils misleads.

The most important similarity between the *Belladonna* and *Fireflies* is this. Because Renaissance people did not have access to the relevant studies, those who used belladonna could not have intended to give this false impression. They thought that what makes them more attractive are larger pupils *qua* larger pupils in the sense in which blue eyes *qua* blue eyes may make a person pretty. They knew that they would look prettier by dilating pupils, but they did not know *why*. Therefore, they intended *only* the result (looking more attractive). Not realising that you are being deceptive by behaving in a certain way is important because you cannot intend to generate X by φ-ing if you do not know that φ-ing generates X. If a person does not know that using belladonna causes a misleading impression, that is, she cannot intend or expect to cause it (compare, Krstić, 2020b, 2023b) and, thus, she cannot intend to mislead. Therefore, these women engaged in deception, but they did not intend to mislead. They thought that their dilated pupils were a sign of beauty just as the predator Photuris fireflies 'think' that their signal means 'Food, come down'.

Let us analyse *Belladonna* by considering a passage from Davidson (1963: 686–687), who writes [italics and a comment added]:

> I flip the switch, turn on the light, and illuminate the room. Unbeknownst to me I also alert a prowler to the fact that I am home. Here I do not do four things, but only one, of which four descriptions have been given. I flipped the switch because I wanted to turn on the light, and by saying I wanted to turn on the light I explain (give my reason for, rationalize) the flipping [I flipped the switch because I intended to turn on the light, rem. a]. But I do not ... rationalize my alerting of the prowler *nor my illuminating of the room*.

What rationalises dilating pupils is that the Renaissance women want to look more attractive (they intend the result). Just as Davidson flips the switch *to* illuminate the room, they use belladonna *to* look more attractive. However, flipping the switch does not directly illuminate the room; rather, one illuminates the room *by* turning on the light. Likewise, unbeknownst to everyone, dilating pupils does not directly make a person look more attractive; rather, people with dilated pupils look more attractive *by* causing the relevant misleading impression. And just as the function of turning on the light is to illuminate the room, the function of using belladonna is to cause this misleading impression. Therefore, we have deception when dilating pupils misleads, just as we illuminate the room when we flip the switch.

However, unlike Davidson, who knows that he will illuminate the room by turning on the light, which is why he intends to turn on the light, and unlike myself who expects to get your money by causing you to falsely believe that your dead Nigerian uncle left you a fortune, Renaissance women did not know that they would look prettier by giving this false impression. Rather, they thought that flipping the switch (dilating pupils) directly illuminated the room (made them look prettier) without the 'mediation' of turning on the light (misleading). Therefore, they intended only to illuminate the room (look prettier) by flipping the switch (dilating pupils); they did not intend to deceive (turn on the light).

Similar behaviour occurs in contemporary society as well. Some people put on makeup so subtly that it looks like they are not wearing makeup at all. Because the function of this behaviour typically is to cause false beliefs about one's appearance and age, they are engaged in deception, but we should not think that they all intend to mislead. Most of them simply do this because it is fashionable, because they want to look younger, and so on. They do not intend or expect to mislead.

Before I proceed, I need to resolve some objections to my argument.

2.2.3 Resolving Some Concerns

The way to know whether the function of behaviours of people putting on makeup or 'not being themselves' job candidates is to mislead or something like 'securing my practical interests' is to identify the behaviour's proximal function in the relevant context. If securing my practical interests is the proximal function of my behaviour or trait, then I do not count as engaging in deception and the epistemic harm was caused by an accident or a mistake. However, if the practical interests are being secured by misleading, then misleading is the function of my behaviour (it is the most proximal activity in the sequence) and securing these practical interests is its result.

One worry may be that my main argument is viciously circular: I use cases of supposed non-paradigmatic deception to support my analysis of human deception, but I then use my analysis to argue that these cases involve deception. Therefore, I will show that theories of biological deception also classify my cases as involving deception and that each case has its clear analogue in animal deception.

Skyrmsian analysis counts my cases as deception: the signals are false, the senders systematically benefit from sending them, and the receivers suffer harm and are misled. Even though job interviews are performances, they are the kind of performances that should be reliable indicators of the candidates' real qualities. Therefore, job candidates can transmit false signals and these signals systematically bring benefit to some of them when the committee is misled or harmed (by hiring a 'not-perfect' candidate). Also, when people put on makeup or dilate pupils, they transmit false signals regarding their appearance and these signals systematically bring them benefit when they mislead or harm the receivers. Therefore, this is all deception.

Birch's strategic exploitation view also counts them as deception. According to this view (Birch, 2019: 31), a signal S, sent in a state of the world X, is biologically deceptive iff:

(a) Sending S in X elicits some behaviour B in the receiver.
(b) S elicits B in X not because B benefits the receiver in X, but because (i) B benefits receivers in some other state of the world, X', and (ii) $P(X'|S) > P(X')$.
(c) S is sent in X as part of a strategy.
(d) The sender's strategy has been maintained by selection, at least in part, because of the payoffs conferred by the receiver's performance of B in X.

In this state of the world X, at least for some members of the search committee, the candidate's behaviour raises the subjective probability of a non-actual state of the world X' in which the candidate is perfect for the job, and search committees hire candidates (behaviour B) when they are in X'. This behaviour is part of a strategy that has been maintained by selection, at least in part, because of the payoffs conferred by search committee members' performance of B in X: candidates present themselves as the perfect candidate because this is who search committees hire. Therefore, this is deception.

Similarly, in this state of the world X, dilating pupils raises the subjective probability of a non-actual state of the world X' in which the person is more attractive, and people tend to look (more) favourably (behaviour B) on people when they are in X'. These behaviours involve a strategy maintained by selection, at least in part, because of the payoffs conferred by other people's performance of B in X: people improve their appearance because this allows them to leave a (more) positive visual impression on others (the payoff). Therefore, this is deception.

These examples also have clear analogues in biological deception. In a commonly discussed kind of automimicry, some members of a species resemble their better-defended conspecifics. One example is the Monarch butterfly (*Danaus Plexippus*): some monarchs do not contain toxic cardiac glycosides, but predators cannot easily know which ones do. This is how job candidates mimic perfect candidates. Similarly, some animals have colouration on their head that makes their horns and antlers look bigger or their ears are positioned next to horns to make it look like the animal has more horns (Guthrie and Petocz, 1970; West-Eberhard, 1979: 226) and some plants give an impression of more extensive thorns by having colourful elongated organs found in some plants (Lev-Yadun, 2003). These organisms are not misrepresenting themselves as someone else. Rather, the function of colouration, ears, or fake thorns is to exaggerate the already existing qualities: they make the horns look bigger or give the impression that the organism has more horns or thorns. Using the belladonna extract or putting on makeup is analogous to these cases: their function is to exaggerate an individual's existing qualities.

In conclusion, these cases involve deception on other theories of biological deception, and they have clear analogues in animal deception. Therefore, intending to deceive is not necessary for interpersonal deception. The time has come to present the functional analysis of self-deception.

3 A Functional Analysis of Self-Deception

3.1 The Theory

In paradigmatic human deception, deceivers aim for a specific result *by* misleading; both the result and the means of achieving it (i.e., misleading) are intended. In non-paradigmatic human deception, deceivers aim for a specific result by behaving in a specific way, but they do not realise that they achieve this result by misleading; only the result is intended. Finally, deceptive behaviour is sometimes strategic ('If in context C, perform behaviour φ / activate trait Φ') and triggered automatically, without thorough conscious deliberation regarding possible consequences. These deceivers do not consciously aim for a specific result but are rather automatically and pre-consciously responding to a certain stimulus. Neither the result nor misleading is intended.

I think that something similar to non-paradigmatic interpersonal deception normally happens in self-deception. The need to generate a specific result – for example, the need to satisfy a desire that p is true (Roz loves me) or that p comes about (my favourite team wins), reduce anxiety, dissonance, and so on – sets in motion a behaviour (activates a trait) whose function in the given context is to mislead about *whether p*. The desire triggers this specific behaviour (trait) because misleading about *whether p* is the best (or the only) way to generate this result. Even when the agent consciously 'wants' the result (e.g., to reduce anxiety), they are not intentionally deceiving themselves; they do not realise that their behaviour misleads. Therefore, no paradoxes arise (see, Krstić forthcoming: §4). Self-deception can also be strategic in the sense in which it simply is an automatic response to a certain stimulus, in which case the trigger (stimulus) rather than the result explains why the person engages in self-deception.

The function of the relevant behaviour/trait is to mislead in a certain context (§2.2.2). It is neither to mislead the self specifically nor to mislead always. Deception need not be directed at some specific target. A politician may lie on national television hoping to mislead someone, anyone. And, because it models self-deception on interpersonal deception, my analysis preserves this feature.

Also, a deceptive behaviour such as playing dead can have the function to mislead in one context (e.g., while facing a bear) but not in another (e.g., while acting in a play). Shakespeare's Juliet deceives Romeo by playing dead even though she does not intend to deceive him. In contrast, an actress rehearsing for her role of Juliet may merely mislead a passer-by unaware of the context. What we now get is the following.

By φ-ing or exhibiting a trait Φ in a certain context, S deceives themselves iff the function of φ-ing (Φ) in this context is to mislead *and* φ-ing (exhibiting Φ) causally contributes to S's ending up misled. When φ-ing (exhibiting Φ) generates a further result, it generates it non-deviantly by misleading. The following analysis should be capable of capturing all possible cases of self-deception, intentional, unintentional, and non-intentional. (Allow me to focus on behaviours for the sake of simplicity.)

For every subject S, proposition *p*, context C, and action φ, S has deceived himself *about p* in C by φ-ing iff

(1) S φ-s in context C due to an influence of a desire, emotion, or interest, or as a part of a (non-conscious) strategy,
(2) The function of φ-ing in C is to mislead,
(3) By φ-ing in C, S is 'not being itself' – since S normally does not φ in C,
(4) (In part) because of (2), S becomes misled *about whether p*.

- *If* φ-ing generates a further result (e.g., satisfies the relevant desire, emotion, or interest), this result is (better) performed by φ-ing rather than by what S normally does in C.

Conditions 1–4 are necessary and sufficient for self-deception. The further condition (•) is not necessary (§4.3); however, because it is commonly satisfied in self-deception, it should be discussed. Szabados (1974: 57), Barnes (1997), and Holton (2001: 55–56) correctly argue that self-deceivers must be misled about a subject matter, that is, *whether p*, rather than just in believing one proposition (also, Galeotti, 2018; Wehofsits, 2023: 8, n. 21). Just like regular dupes, self-deceivers can be misled about *whether p* in many ways. Normally, *p* is false and they believe it as true; however, *p* can be true but their credence in *p* could be inaccurate, they could falsely believe that believing that *p* is justified, that they used the right reasoning method when answering the question *whether p*, that they did not assess evidence in a biased way, that they have nothing at stake in this debate, and so on. And deception can even spread to related areas (Funkhouser and Hallam, 2024: 19). A mother who deceives herself about her son's smoking pot may start deceiving herself about why she suddenly stopped cleaning his room (where she might find the pot).

My account does not contain some conditions or involve some hypotheses standardly associated with self-deception. For example, it says nothing about the available evidence or the relevant epistemic standard of reasoning. I do not deny that self-deceivers typically end up with epistemically unjustified beliefs. I just argue that this need not happen (§3.2). A discomfort, dissonance, or behavioural tension can arise in self-deception, but their presence is not necessarily a sign that self-deceivers 'deep down' know the truth or that they are intentionally deceiving themselves; rather, it is a sign that they suspect that they are not being their regular self (§3.2). Finally, while I do think that some people deceive themselves intentionally, these are not the 'classic cases' of self-deception.

My account appears similar to some other views, but this is only in appearance. Consider the way Mele (e.g. 2001, 2020) uses the FTL (*F*riedrich, *T*rope, *L*iberman) account of lay hypothesis testing to explain self-deception (Friedrich, 1993; Trope and Liberman, 1996). According to FTL, hypothesis testing aims to avoid the primary error, which is a costly false belief. The costs of false positives and false negatives are asymmetric, and the primary error is the costlier belief. Which beliefs are costlier (i.e., primary error) depends on our desires and interests (Friedrich, 1993; see, Scott-Kakures, 2000). Therefore, a person with some powerful interests at stake may require a lot of evidence to conclude that p (believing that p would be the perceived primary error) but only some trivial evidence to conclude that not-p. In turn, this person may come to believe that not-p in a biased fashion (the bias shifted the thresholds towards believing that not-p), this behaviour will have a functional description, and the belief that not-p will be false.

This behaviour, however, does not involve self-deception in my view because misleading is not the function of the FTL. The FTL-based analysis explains the possession of the false belief by the biasing effects of desire, which changes the relevant thresholds: Because of the motivational bias, the process that generates the epistemic harm is not intentional, but if the subject's reasoning is sensitive to her desires or interests rather than to the facts or the truth, then she comes to believe as she does regardless of the truth of the matter. Acquiring the relevant belief is not an accident, that is. However, while not reasoning based on your evidence increases the probability of making an error, it does not negate the fact that this will essentially still be an error. Therefore, the presence of the bias means only that the person did not mislead herself by accident, but the fact remains that she misled herself by mistake (i.e., error).

Likewise, according to dissonance reduction deflationary account (Scott-Kakures, 2009, 2021), certain attitudes are resistant to change and, when threatened, they (pre-consciously) trigger various forms of rationalisation and biased inquiry. Because the function of this behaviour is re-establishing the consistency of cognitive attitudes, its function is not to mislead and the coming to believe what is false or at odds with available evidence is a mistake. Now, having mentioned dissonance reduction, one may respond that there is a sense in which self-deception could be called a mistake. Many self-deceivers take themselves to be trying to rid themselves of uncertainty. Therefore, from their perspective, their self-deception is a mistake – notwithstanding how much their conclusion that p might be welcome. 'What was I thinking!' a self-deceiver may think in the aftermath of her self-deception's being revealed.

Do not be misled by this reaction: even if we could call self-deception a mistake, it is not the kind of a mistake that undermines the characterisation of something as deception. We need to distinguish an organism *causing* X by accident or a mistake from X *being* an accident or a mistake. Juliet misleads Romeo by accident: because of the plague, the messenger who should inform Romeo cannot leave Verona, and Romeo never learns about her plan. Even though *Juliet* misleads Romeo by accident, *misleading Romeo* is not an accident or a mistake: Juliet's behaviour performs its function perfectly well in this context. Juliet determines all the factors necessary and sufficient for anyone who sees her to end up misled. She just fails to determine all the factors necessary and sufficient to make sure that Romeo is not misled. Her failure to determine these latter factors is the mistake she makes. What I mean is that her mistake is that she does not make sure that Romeo does not get deceived, but there is no mistake when Romeo is misled; this is what her playing dead is supposed to do. Surely, upon waking up, she could cry out 'What was I thinking? Why did I ever come up with such a terrible plan?' Her regret is no evidence that she did not engage in deception. Her regret is evidence that she should have been more cautious. The self-deceiver's cry 'What was I thinking!' makes sense because their mistake is like the one made by Juliet. They should have been more careful.

My view should also not be confused with Johnston's (1988) view. According to Johnston (1988), what causes self-deception is a non-accidental but non-rational direct connection between a desire and a belief. Johnston calls this subintentional, purpose-serving mental mechanism *mental tropism*. In self-deception, the anxiety that the person's desire that p will not be satisfied is reduced by her ceasing to acknowledge her own recognition of information that suggests that not-p (this is *repression*) while her subsequent acquisition of the belief that p, made possible by repressing the conflicting information, is based on her desire to believe it (this is *wishful thinking*). These processes typically serve to reduce anxiety (Johnston, 1988: 86). Repression alleviates the stress of believing the unfavourable proposition, whereas wishful thinking aims to acquire the desired belief – since repressing the belief that not-*p* does not entail acquiring the belief that *p*. The desire that *p*, having no obstacles due to repression, then directly, purposefully, non-rationally, and non-intentionally generates the belief that *p*. However, even though tropisms serve a function, that function is not to mislead. Therefore, when they mislead, this is a mistake (i.e., an event that departs from the tropism's purpose).

My functional analysis is also, in important ways, different from Livingstone Smith's (2014) *teleofunctional* analysis of self-deception. Livingstone Smith (2014: 190) defines deception as:

> For organisms O1 and O2, O1 deceives O2 iff O2 possesses a character C with the purpose F of representing some feature of its world accurately and O1 possesses a character C* with purpose F* of causing C to misrepresent that feature, and it is in virtue of performing F* that C* causes C to misrepresent that feature.

Both views understand the function of the thing that misleads as misleading: the purpose of C* is to cause C to misrepresent some feature of the world. However, one fundamental difference is that while the functional view models self-deception on interpersonal deception, the teleofunctional analysis models it on biological deception. Therefore, the two views offer two importantly different solutions to the existing problems. Another difference is that the teleofunctional view sees deception as a one-to-one relationship: C*'s purpose is connected to C and the corresponding feature of the world. The functional view involves a one-to-many relationship: the function of φ or Φ is to mislead regarding a subject matter (*whether p*), and it may target any aspect of this subject matter. Also, some 'characters' (C) do not have the purpose (F) of representing some feature of the world accurately, and the deceiver can exploit them to manipulate the victim and deceive her. The function of consonance-restoring mechanisms or mental tropisms is to restore consonance or reduce anxiety rather than to represent the world accurately, but a skilful deceptive manipulator can use them to mislead.

Finally, my account only requires that the function of the behaviour/trait involved in (self-)deception is to mislead. It does not assume that misleading must generate some result, that is, have a *telos*. According to Livingstone Smith's (2014: 195–197) or Johnston's (1988) analyses, self-deception must generate some benefit to the agent (this is its telos); however, in many cases, self-deception does not benefit the agent, some instances are not adaptive, and some are even maladaptive (Van Leeuwen, 2009; Funkhouser, 2017, 2019: 242–244; Krstić, 2021). Just consider parents who deceived themselves into believing that they are to blame for their child's death although the child died of leukaemia. This behaviour does not seem to be bringing any benefit, perceived or real, to them.

I will discuss the idea that self-deception must have a 'telos' in detail in §4. Here, I need to say that I do not intend to argue that self-deceptive behaviour generates no results or cannot generate them. Rather, I argue (i) that sometimes the result cannot explain *why* we have self-deception in the way in which deterring predators explains why the Western hog-nosed snake plays dead and (ii) that sometimes self-deception generates no results. In short, in addition to the garden-variety cases, my view is designed to capture cases of self-deception:

(a) that once generated beneficial results in C but now generate results that are not beneficial or even detrimental, and vice versa,
(b) that generate beneficial results in some contexts but are triggered by the same stimuli in contexts in which they *cannot* generate (beneficial) results (a heart may beat even when separated from the blood vessels), or
(c) that are based on behaviour/trait that evolved because misleading *others* systematically generates some result but *not* because misleading the *self* generates some result (weak crayfish have large claws because this deters opponents, not because it misleads themselves),
(d) in which the person's response is strategic and non-intentional.

For instance, deceiving oneself into believing that one does not have some potentially fatal illness might have been beneficial in the past, since it would allow one to at least live one's remaining days with less stress, but now it may just prevent the sufferer from acquiring a life-saving treatment – an example of (a). This is a one-person analogue of Juliet deceiving Romeo. Romeo's appearance changes the circumstances but not the context, and as a result, an adaptive behaviour (playing dead) now backfires. And some kinds of self-deception may have been transformed from maladaptive to adaptive by a change in historical circumstances. The behaviour whereby a man deceives himself into believing that his wife is not having an affair may have been maladaptive in the past since the affair would have increased the chances of his genes not being transferred to their children. However, with the invention of contraception, deceiving oneself for the sake of preserving one's marriage might be adaptive – an example of (a) vice versa.

Perhaps it is beneficial to deceive oneself into believing that one's partner is not having an affair, but the same mechanism could be triggered regarding some distant else's partner. In this case, the mechanism was triggered by accident or by mistake, since this result does not explain why the mechanism was selected, but misleading is not a mistake nonetheless. Similarly, just as the heart may beat even when separated from the blood vessels, self-deceptive behaviour may be triggered in a context in which it is possible to mislead the self but impossible to generate the relevant further result. These examples all fall into category (b). Also, people standardly rationalise evidence in order to cause *others* to believe what they want them to believe, but people like Sid can deceive themselves in the same way – an example of (c). Finally, some people may simply be engaging in self-deception in the way fireflies engage in deception: automatically and triggered by an unconscious strategy, we may even identify this as a habit – an example of (d).

One may think that the existence of non-adaptive or maladaptive self-deception is a problem for the functional view, since one may expect such behaviour to be deselected: without the beneficial result, it is unclear what causes the person to engage in self-deception. However, there is no need to think that every trait, disposition, or behaviour that persists is adaptive or that any strategic behaviour generates results. Perhaps the evolutionary processes just need some time to deselect them: self-inflation bias is not adaptive, but contemporary society tolerates it (Funkhouser, 2019: §7) – and some relevant historical circumstances may facilitate or tolerate them. Consider the so-called 'nervous' or 'fainting' goats.

When nervous goats are suddenly surprised or startled, they become perfectly rigid. This condition usually lasts only ten to twenty seconds, but it is still not adaptive to freeze in the face of danger when this is not a strategy of avoiding predators. However, farmers keep these goats because they cannot jump over fences; they freeze if they try. The farmers, that is, turned this maladaptive disposition into an adaptive disposition: this disability actually gives these goats an advantage over those who can jump over fences. Also, some pointer dogs exhibit sudden immobility in the presence of humans. And while the dog owners do not welcome this behaviour in the way farmers welcome the behaviour of nervous goats, they do not see it as a reason not to have these dogs (Krstić, 2021, 2023c).

Similarly, human infants exhibit maladaptive heightened fearfulness, essentially a deceptive trait: the function of heightened fearfulness is to mislead, just as the function of dilating pupils is to mislead. And just as Western hog-nosed snakes simulate death because this deters predators, human infants exhibit heightened fearfulness because it leads to being helped and protected (Grossmann, 2023: §2). However, since the fear is exaggerated, the response is also exaggerated, and because exaggerated reactions require using unnecessary resources, this behaviour is, technically, maladaptive. Luckily, however, humans are ultra-social, and they can afford to allocate unnecessary resources. Thus, the heightened fear in children continues to persist; human social structure is capable of mitigating or even annulling its negative effects (Krstić, 2023c).

All in all, my functional view contains the following important ideas. First, a satisfactory analysis of self-deception cannot assume that it is a mistake or a mere accident that the self-deceiver is misled. The *conditio sine qua non* is that the function of the behaviour or the trait that misleads is to mislead. I have defended this thesis thus far. Because functional analysis can capture both the cases of intentional and non-intentional human deception, and because it does not generate paradoxes when applied to self-deception, it should be preferred. Second, self-deception is a kind of internal irrationality: self-deceivers are 'not being themselves'. I proceed to defend this thesis next. The third important thesis is that self-deception need not be adaptive. I will defend it in §4.

3.2 Self-Deception as Not Being Yourself

3.2.1 Introduction

Because not all self-deceivers deceive themselves by behaving in obviously deceptive ways, it would be natural to spell out some deceptive behaviours and traits. This is something I cannot do, but for a very good reason: context partially determines whether a certain behaviour or trait is deceptive (§2.2.1, §3.1) and, thus, what might be an honest behaviour in some contexts will have a deceptive character in others. Because, in the right circumstances, pretty much any trait or behaviour can be used to deceive – even sending true messages (Krstić and Saville, 2019; Krstić, 2024ca, 2025) – and because I model self-deception on interpersonal deception, pretty much any behaviour or trait can be self-deceptive in my view. So, how to identify self-deception, then? This section tries to answer this question.

Philosophers predominantly think that self-deceivers cause themselves to acquire or retain incorrect and epistemically unjustified beliefs (credence in propositions) and, on the most popular view, we can identify self-deceivers by comparing their beliefs with beliefs their impartial cognitive peers, ICPs, would form (Mele, 2001: 106–107, 2009: 146–147; Lynch, 2012; Dolcini, 2016; similarly, Galeotti, 2018: 45). If most of the ICPs would examine the same evidence using as much reflection on the same issue as her and form a different belief, the person is deceiving herself.

I think that we should instead compare how a person *normally* reasons with how she reasons *now*. If we have reasons to think that, due to some motivating factor, she does not behave the way she normally behaves, then we should ascribe self-deception to her even if we or her ICPs think that her belief is epistemically justified. Self-deception is characterised by a kind of motivated internal irrationality: the person is being inconsistent; she is not behaving as she normally does. And because this kind of irrationality can be identified from the outside – namely, we can notice that self-deceivers do not behave the way they normally behave – we can identify self-deception by seeing whether the person is not being herself.

An immediate worry with this proposal is the issue of whether we have a grasp of how an individual typically behaves sufficient to identify self-deception by noting the departure from this behaviour. We often have no experience or history with those to whom we attribute self-deception. I think that we should not ascribe self-deception to those whom we do not know well enough. More importantly, if we have no experience or history with the person, then we do not know how she typically reasons and, thus, we cannot identify her genuine ICPs. This is why most scholars take the ICP criterion rather loosely. Instead of looking for genuine ICPs, we use ourselves as a model of epistemic 'rectitude': given the evidence, here is what (we think) should be believed. And the notable difference is interest or desire: but for the motivational states, the individual is not likely to have come to believe what they believe; rather, they would have believed what *I think* they should believe. I fear that this is a recipe for false positives. And even if we try to find the person's ICPs is sometimes rather dangerous. Consider the case of Ignaz Semmelweis.

> *Ignaz* was a Hungarian physician who discovered that the incidence of childbed fever could be drastically reduced by requiring healthcare workers in obstetrical clinics to disinfect their hands. His procedures led to a significant drop in the maternal death rate in his clinic. However, because his observations conflicted with the established medical theories of that time, his ideas were rejected and ridiculed by the medical community. Some doctors were even offended at the suggestion that they should wash their hands and mocked him for it. Ignaz insisted on his view, contacting everyone he could contact. Four years after the publication of his book, he started exhibiting neurotic behaviour caused by constant ridicule and his ruined image and career, which ended with a series of nervous breakdowns. Eventually, he was lured into an asylum where he was locked up and beaten up by the guards. He died 14 days later from a gangrenous wound likely caused by the beating.

Notice, it is perfectly natural to think that the members of the relevant medical community were Ignaz's ICPs. True, some of them were offended and thus perhaps not impartial, but their view had overwhelming evidential and theoretic support at that time. It was just that the evidence was misleading and the theories used to explain it were false. On the view that the belief Ignaz's ICPs would form is the benchmark against which we would judge whether Ignaz is a self-deceiver (i.e., whether he exhibits the appropriate motivation), we get a clear false positive here. Therefore, we have a good reason not to rely on the ICP test in such a context: it may misclassify people who jump out of the system as being self-deceived.

The idea that self-deception involves motivated internal irrationality is not novel. Davidson (1986) famously insists that self-deception involves a person violating her own norms. Similarly, Szabados (1974) mentions that self-deception involves quasi-rationality. Michel and Newen (2010) suggest that self-deception involves applying double standards in evaluating beliefs relevant to one's self-esteem: the person's belief-evaluation method depends on the anticipated result rather than on the assessment of the method itself. Finally, on Mele's account (1987, 1997, 2001, 2020), because they treat (seemingly) relevant data in a motivationally biased way, self-deceivers do not reason the way they normally reason.

Because we are not being our regular selves when we reason in a biased way, it may seem that I am merely reformulating a widely shared hypothesis. However, this appearance is misleading. I also argue that self-deceivers need not end up with epistemically unjustified mental states, their reasoning need not be normatively faulty, and it need not deviate from the reasoning of their ICPs. The bias can even improve the self-deceiver's reasoning by trumping a systematically exhibited reasoning failure. This is something most philosophers straightforwardly deny. For example, Barnes (1997: 78) writes that 'as a result of this bias in the self-deceiver's belief-acquisition process, the self-deceiver's belief that p is never justified[;] [the] self-deceiver will never have adequate grounds for thinking that his or her belief that p is true' (similarly, Van Leeuwen, 2009: 112; Dolcini, 2016; Galeotti, 2018: 52).

I am not advocating for a radical break-up with the idea that self-deceptive beliefs are epistemically problematic. I just want to modify it. Even when the self-deceiver's belief is epistemically unjustified, it is unjustified because the person does not behave how she normally behaves. Also, I do not deny that self-deception is a failure to believe in accordance with one's evidence. I just argue that what counts as one's evidence is not for us or one's ICPs to decide. One's evidence should be determined based on how one normally reasons. When people come to see that they have self-deceived themselves and regret it, what they regret is that they had failed to mind the evidence. And they regret not being themselves because they take themselves as possessing the competence to respond to evidence appropriately. Importantly, they may think that they possess this competence even if everyone else thinks differently; this was surely true of Ignaz.

I now proceed to present my theoretical apparatus and then argue that my view should be preferred.

3.2.2 Not Being Yourself

Davidson (1985) famously distinguishes when a mental state or action is irrational or incoherent from *the third-person perspective*, which is when a person has a set of attitudes that are inconsistent with someone else's standards, from when it is irrational from *the first-person perspective*, which is when her attitudes are inconsistent by her own standards. Let us call this first-person kind of irrationality (inconsistency) *internal*.

I argue that internal irrationality characterises self-deception even though self-deceivers need not realise that they are misleading themselves. They may, nonetheless, notice that they are not behaving the way they would normally behave, and when they do notice this, they will exhibit some discomfort, doxastic dissonance, or behavioural tension, they may avoid some evidence, and so on. However, the cause of this discomfort or tension is not the realisation that they simultaneously believe that p and that not-p, but rather the feeling that they are doing something they typically would not do. I do not argue that no self-deceiver 'knows the truth deep down'. Rather, I argue that, for the tension, dissonance, or discomfit to arise, it is sufficient that the person thinks, suspects, or 'feels inside' that she is not really being her normal self. This would also make her avoid some evidence since the evidence will remind her of her own inconsistency. Let us now draw three uncontroversial insights from the proposed distinction between external and internal irrationality.

First, a 'third person' can reliably judge that a mental state or action is first-person irrational: *you* can judge that *my* mental state or behaviour is internally irrational even when *I* fail to notice this. To identify internal irrationality from the outside, we need to focus on how the person normally reasons as opposed to how she reasons now, rather than on whether she is violating some epistemic norms or laws of logic (i.e., whether she is externally irrational). 'Is she being herself?' we should ask. If we suspect that the person is not really herself, an outward sign of internal irrationality, we should suspect that she is deceiving herself. The reason for this approach lies in the second insight.

Second, in certain situations, my mental state or action can be rational from the third-person perspective (external rationality) while being irrational from the first-person perspective (internal irrationality). I call this mental state or action *pseudo-rational* since it is normatively rational but subjectively irrational. It is normatively rational because it satisfies the normative standards of reasoning: people from my environment reason or behave in such a way. And it is subjectively irrational because those are not *my* standards: I am 'not being myself' (I am being internally incoherent) even if I do not notice it. Notice, when I say that those are not 'my' standards, I do not mean that a person who, for example, systematically jumps to conclusions endorses jumping to conclusions. Rather, she jumps to conclusions thinking that this is the correct way to reason in the given context. She endorses this behaviour not knowing that her reasoning is erroneous.

Third, the self-deceiver's 'not being oneself' is analogous to the 'not being oneself' of the Belladonna women or the predator female firefly. The predator female firefly does what she normally does when she 'wants' to eat; she is being regular herself in *this* sense. However, she is not being regular herself in the sense that she is misrepresenting herself as someone else, namely, as a sexually receptive ('honest') female. By analogy, self-deceivers are being their normal selves in the sense that they may standardly engage in self-deception in certain contexts, but they are not being their normal selves in the sense that this is not how they would normally behave had they not been motivated to believe a certain proposition. Because the 'not being oneself' of the self-deceiver preserves the analogy between self-deception and other-deception and since this kind of irrationality can be detected from the outside, this is the best way to identify self-deception. I now proceed to defend this position.

3.2.3 The Argument

According to the most popular view, the way to identify the level of emotional or motivational bias appropriate for a person self-deceived about something – that is, the way to identify a self-deceiver – is to see what kind of belief the person's ICPs would acquire or retain. If the majority of her ICPs would examine the same evidence using as much reflection on the same issue as her, and conclude that her belief is false, we can say that the person is a self-deceiver. Impartial cognitive peers are people very similar to the person being tested in things such as education and intelligence, but who do not have an emotional stake in the issue at hand, who do not desire any relevant proposition to be true, and who would not prefer any evidence over some other evidence (Mele, 2009: 146–147).

I argue that focusing on whether the person is not being herself is a better way to identify self-deception. My argument involves discussing five cases, starting with *Ben*.

> *Ben*: Say that Ben systematically commits reasoning fallacy F (e.g., jumps to conclusions) in context C, but that humans systematically do *not* commit F in C. However, a consequence of making F in C now is that the available evidence strongly suggests that Ben's partner is having an affair (p). Due to his strong desire that his partner is *not* having an affair (not-p) and *not* because he objectively recognizes the available data's evidential goodness, Ben acquires the relevant belief that not-p now by way of not committing F in C (i.e., by not reasoning the way he normally reasons in C) and he, therefore, ends up with the belief humans systematically end up with in C. Unfortunately, while epistemically justified, this belief is false: Ben's partner is having an affair.

C is a context in which Ben makes inferences to the best explanation regarding people's behaviour. Because Ben systematically jumps to conclusions in C, we get that Ben systematically makes faulty inferences to the best explanation when interpreting other people's behaviour, and his relevant beliefs are systematically unjustified. However, this time, C involves assessing the behaviour of Ben's partner concerning a very sensitive topic. If Ben were to jump to a conclusion, he would infer that she is having an affair. However, because he desperately wants it to be true that his partner is not having an affair, Ben exhibits a reasoning bias. And the bias cannot simply make Ben's poor reasoning worse, since this would only make him more confident in the proposition he does not want to be true. Rather, because jumping to conclusions in C leads to a proposition Ben does not want to be true, the bias must improve his reasoning so that he now carefully evaluates all the evidence and avoids making the conclusion he does not want to be true. Ben's reasoning now is pseudo-rational: it is normatively rational but internally irrational. And because they do not jump to conclusions in C, Ben's friends form the same belief as Ben.

One might object that because Ben's reasoning appears to differ systematically from that of other humans, these humans are not his ICPs. Ben's real ICPs would commit F in C and would, thus, not share Ben's views. Therefore, the ICP test succeeds; we just need to find Ben's real ICPs. I am not sure that ICPs must think just like unbiased Ben, but instead of defending this view, I ask: if Ben's IPCs need to think *just like* unbiased Ben, why do we need them? We just need to consider what Ben would normally conclude in this context, had his bias been absent. We need to know this if we want to find his ICPs anyway. So, seeing that Ben is not being his regular self comes before identifying his ICPs.

The 'not being yourself' hypothesis also preserves a nice analogy with other-deception. Ben acts like a person who systematically does not jump to conclusions because this satisfies his desire, just as the predator female firefly acts like an 'honest' female because this brings her food. To get what they 'want', both deceivers must not be themselves: Ben will not believe the welcome proposition if he continues to jump to conclusions, and males will not descend if the predator sends a signal that means 'I am hungry and I need you to come down'. Importantly, Ben's false belief is luckily epistemically justified and consistent with the belief that his friends also formed. Because Ben now considers all his evidence, the assessment of his environment cannot tell us whether he deceived himself in C or not. Therefore, analyses based on the idea that self-deceivers end up with unjustified beliefs will not classify this as self-deception.

My functional view classifies this as self-deception. Not only that Ben's belief that not-p is false, he is also misled about which standard of reasoning he would normally use in C and about the reason why he is deviating from his typical reasoning. Therefore, Ben is deceived *about whether p* – condition 4.

Had Ben reasoned the way he usually does, he would reach p (affair!) rather than not-p; he is 'not being himself' – condition 3. And just as the predator female firefly can lure the honest males only by not being herself, Ben can end up believing that not-p only by not jumping to conclusion, which explains why he 'is not being himself' and gives us good reasons to say that the function of his behaviour is to mislead – condition 2. Ben's 'not being himself' is a one-person analogue of the behaviour of women using belladonna or predator female fireflies; they are all not being themselves. Satisfying Ben's desire that his partner is not having an affair (condition 1) is the result of this behaviour, and this result explains why Ben engages in self-deception.

One may argue that even if Ben is propositionally justified in believing that his partner is not having an affair (he has good reasons to believe this), he is not doxastically justified in so believing (he does not form his belief based on those reasons) – since he is self-deceived *in coming* to believe that his partner is not having an affair. Therefore, the belief is not sufficiently justified, and the idea that self-deceivers always fall below some epistemic standard is salvaged. However, the fact that Ben is self-deceived in coming to believe that not-p is consistent with the fact that he forms his false belief from good reasons. The description of the case is such that the bias shifts Ben's reasoning towards good reasons; the bias causally contributes towards the belief being doxastically justified. To this, one may respond that if Ben is moved to believe based on a normatively apt grasp of epistemic considerations, he is not self-deceived. This does not follow for two reasons.

First, Ben does not recognise the evidential goodness of the data he assesses. He assesses it in this particular way because he wants that not-p is true. If he were to reason the way he reasons when he is not biased, he would treat the same data differently: he would jump to a conclusion and believe that p. The bias involved in this case is the same kind of bias we see in paradigmatic cases of self-deception; the only difference is that the bias applies to a person who systematically reasons erroneously. Second, the fact that the belief is based on good reasons does not suggest that this is not (self-)deception: Romeo's belief that Juliet was dead was also justified, both doxastically and propositionally. In trying to understand the cases from this section, one should think outside the standard 'self-deception' box and within the 'interpersonal deception' box. This standard 'self-deception' box is too small and often confusing.

Consider now the cases of *Mario*, his twin brother *Dario*, and their ICPs.

> *Mario*: Say that humans systematically commit a reasoning fallacy F in context C. Say that Mario also systematically commits F in C but that, sadly, making F in C now generates the true conclusion 'My partner *is* having an affair'. Due

to a strong influence of the desire that his partner is *not* having an affair and not because he recognizes that he tends to reason incorrectly in C, Mario avoids making this conclusion now by reasoning correctly (i.e., by not committing F). And while Mario forms the false belief 'My partner is not having an affair' by reasoning correctly, everyone else forms the true belief that his partner *is* having an affair (p) by reasoning incorrectly (they commit F).

Because they commit F in C but Mario does not, Mario's ICPs would say that he deceived himself into believing that not-p because his belief is epistemically unjustified and false. However, in reality, Mario acquired a belief that is epistemically *justified* but *unluckily* false, whereas his ICPs acquired a belief that is epistemically *unjustified* and *luckily* true. Relying on the judgment of Mario's ICPs causes us to ascribe self-deception to Mario for the wrong reasons. Mario is a self-deceiver for the following reasons. First, his belief that p is false and he is misled about propositions relevant to *whether p* – condition 4. Second, he believes that not-p (no affair) due to the influence of his desire that his partner is not having an affair – condition 1. Third, had he reasoned the way he normally reasons, he would have ended up believing the opposite proposition: Mario is not being himself – condition 3. Fourth, because he is not being himself (the analogy with interpersonal deception), we can plausibly assume that the function of Mario's behaviour is to mislead – condition 2. Thus, this is self-deception in my view.

Consider now Mario's twin brother.

> *Dario*: Say that humans systematically commit F in C and that Dario also systematically commits F in C. However, (unlike in *Mario*) committing this fallacy in C now will generate the *false* conclusion 'My partner *is* having an affair'. Due to a strong influence of the desire that his partner is not having an affair and *not* because he recognizes that he systematically reasons incorrectly in C, Dario avoids making this conclusion by now reasoning correctly in C. Therefore, Dario forms the correct and epistemically justified belief 'My partner is not having an affair' (not-p), whereas everyone else forms the false and epistemically unjustified belief that p.

Again, because they commit F in C but Dario does not, his ICPs would say that Dario is a self-deceiver. However, they would think that Dario is a self-deceiver because his belief is epistemically unjustified and false, but, in fact, *their belief* is epistemically unjustified and false. Rather than focusing on his supposed ICPs or what we think Dario should believe, we should ascribe self-deception to Dario for the following reasons. First, Dario exhibits internal irrationality, condition 3, and his irrationality is motivated – condition 1. Had Dario reasoned the way he usually does, he would reach p (affair) rather than not-p. Second, because he is not being himself and because only not being himself will satisfy his desire, we can plausibly assume that the function of his behaviour is to mislead – condition 2. Finally, just like Ben and Mario, Dario is misled about which standard of reasoning he would normally use in this context and about the reason why he is not behaving the way he normally behaves; he is deceived *about whether p* – condition 4. Therefore, Dario is a self-deceiver.

My final two cases are of two twin sisters, *Anna* and *Hanna*.

> *Anna*: Say that humans systematically commit F in C but that Anna does *not* commit F in C. However, *not committing* F in C now has the consequence of accepting the true proposition 'Anna's partner *is* having an affair' (p), whereas committing it results in accepting the false proposition 'not-p'. Due to her strong desire that her partner is not having an affair, Anna now commits F in C, just like her friends, and they all acquire the false belief that not-p. Anna acquires it because of her strong desire, whereas her friends acquire it because this is how they normally reason in C.

Anna's friends would think that Anna reasoned correctly, but, in fact, she does seem to have deceived herself about her partner's fidelity. Her belief is false and, because she is 'not being herself', we have reasons to believe that she did not mislead herself by mistake or accident; this seems to be the function of her behaviour. If we focus on what we or her friends think Anna should believe in this context, we will not understand her behaviour. However, if we compare how she normally reasons in C with how she reasons now, we will understand everything. Seeing that she is not using the reasoning method she standardly uses, we will know that something is not right; Anna is not being herself. And since she has a good reason for this 'not being herself', we can infer that this reasoning was not an accident or a mistake, which suggests that she is deceiving herself.

Hanna's case is not much different.

> *Hanna*: Say that C involves a situation in which humans systematically *do not* commit F but that Anna's twin sister Hanna commits F in C. Committing F in C now, however, has the consequence of accepting the false proposition 'Hanna's partner is having an affair' (p) whereas not committing it results in accepting the true proposition 'not-p'. Say that due to her strong desire that her partner is not having an affair and not because she recognizes that she systematically reasons incorrectly in C, Hanna now does not commit F in C, just like everyone else, and they all acquire the true belief that not-p. Hanna acquires it because of her strong desire, whereas everyone else acquires it because this is how they normally reason in C.

Even though, unlike her twin Anna, Hanna ends up with a justified true belief that not-p, we have excellent reasons to think that she is a self-deceiver. Just like Dario, she is deceived *about whether p* and she is not being herself. And she is not herself because her desire that a specific proposition is true guides her behaviour. Thus, we have a good reason to think that she did not mislead herself by accident or by mistake. However, because her belief is justified, relying on what we think she should believe gives us a false negative. Thus, in assessing self-deception, we should focus on how the person now behaves as opposed to how she normally behaves.

I end this section by restating my main point. People often engage in fallacious reasoning: they employ rationalisations or reappraisals to justify their views, they doubt the source of threatening information, they shift blame to others or try to explain threatening information or doubts away, they appraise the threatening evidence as ambiguous or support their conclusions with empirical claims that are difficult to verify or falsify, and many more. Engaging in such behaviour is not necessarily self-deceptive since this could just be how they normally behave. However, when the function of such behaviour is to mislead, namely, when this behaviour signals that the person is not being herself, then we can say that she is engaging in self-deception.

More should be said about the cases discussed here, but I will have to do this in follow-up discussions. I now proceed to apply my analysis to *Maria* and *Sid*.

3.3 Explaining *Maria* and *Sid*

Johnny Bravo (Cartoon Network, 1997–2004) consistently interprets female rejections as signs of flirting. This looks like self-deception, but it is not: Johnny simply makes rational inferences from a false premise. Because he firmly believes that he is irresistible, he interprets female rejections as playing hard to get; this is his inference to the best explanation. Johnny is irrational, but only externally. Therefore, to ascribe self-deception to Sid, it is not enough that his belief is false or unjustified: he too could be systematically misinterpreting female rejections by reasoning from a false premise. Rather, we need to know whether Sid standardly rationalises his beliefs in such contexts or only when it comes to Roz. Only in the latter case can we suspect that there is an appropriate motivation involved. And it does seem that this is a one-off thing rather than a systematic tendency to reason incorrectly. What triggers this behaviour is Sid's desire that Roz wants to date him, which causes him to deviate from his normal behaviour. Sid is being internally irrational without noticing it. Therefore, we should understand the case in the following way.

By interpreting Roz's refusal to date him and her reminding him that she has a steady boyfriend as an effort on her part to 'play hard to get', Sid is rationalising his evidence so that it fits the proposition he wants to be true. This behaviour is self-deceptive for the following reasons. Sid rationalises the evidence due to his strong desire – condition 1. Had it been someone else, Sid would have judged that Roz did not want to date this person. Sid is 'not being himself' – condition 3. And because he is 'not being himself', we have reasons to believe that he did not mislead himself accidentally or by mistake; misleading was the function of his behaviour – condition 2. Specifically, Sid cannot be himself if he is to believe that Roz is playing hard to get; thus, he engages in reasoning that will 'bring him' desire satisfaction just as the predator female firefly sends the signal that will bring her food – the result explains why they engage in (self-)deception. Finally, Sid causes himself to end up misled about Roz's intentions, his own motivation, and the justification he has for believing what he believes; he is misled *about whether p* – condition 4. Even if Roz is really playing hard to get, Sid counts as having deceived himself: he is misled about his motive for adopting a specific reasoning method and about his justification for believing what he believes.

Maria is interesting in an important way: it is not clear that Arnold is having an affair. Recall, Arnold has lost sexual interest in Maria, he has protected his phone with a password, and she sometimes picks up what appears to be subtle love signals he exchanges with his female co-actor. This seems like strong evidence that Arnold is having an affair, but this conclusion may be a result of a reasoning error the general population standardly makes in this context; *Maria* could be analogous to *Mario*. The first thing that springs to mind when analysing Arnold's behaviour is 'He is having an affair'. This is the easiest explanation but not necessarily the best explanation. Maria could be perfectly right that Arnold protects his phone with a password because he leaves it on the set while shooting his scenes. Also, bodybuilders often take protein shakes, which increase sexual desire. Not taking proteins would have the appearance of a decreased sexual desire. And exchanging subtle love signals indeed merely reveals flirting, not an affair. Many people flirt without having any further intentions, and innocent flirting is also consistent with Arnold's character; it builds his ego. We could easily be dealing with some random events that merely appear to be connected, in which case the easiest explanation is completely wrong. We are jumping to a conclusion.

None of this is to say that Arnold is not having an affair; rather, the idea is that our analysis of his behaviour could easily be faulty and that, thus, we cannot judge whether Maria is a self-deceiver based on what *we* or her ICPs would have believed in such circumstances. It is not that Maria has no evidence that Arnold is not having an affair but rather that *the ICP assessed evidence that Arnold is having an affair, by itself, is no evidence that Maria is deceiving herself.* In my view, however, we have enough evidence that Maria is deceiving herself even if we do not have enough evidence of the affair.

What gives self-deception away is the difference between how Maria normally interprets this kind of evidence and how she interprets it now. While we and her ICPs are just reasoning the way we normally reason, Maria is not behaving the way she normally would. Had she been reasoning about her friend's husband, she would have judged that he was having an affair. Or had she been reasoning about some other activity of Arnold, she would have been much less diligent in assessing every single possible alternative hypothesis. Her switch in reasoning is the key to identifying self-deception: the switch is motivated by her desire to maintain her belief that Arnold is not having an affair. And, since misleading is the only way of maintaining this belief (the predator firefly can lure harmless males in only by misleading them) and since one must 'not be oneself' to mislead oneself, misleading is not an accident or mistake; this is her behaviour's function. We do not need to know whether Arnold is having an affair. We just need to see whether Maria is being her regular self.

We can also imagine that Sid and Maria feel certain discomfort about their beliefs, or that they exhibit some cognitive dissonance or behavioural tension. Maria could, given the evidence, be uncertain or worried about Arnold's fidelity, and she may stop coming to visit Arnold at work or smell his clothes before washing them – things that used to cause her lots of joy. Philosophers typically discuss tensions that arise between what the person professes to believe and her evidence, or between the person's conscious belief and her (supposed) unconscious belief, or between her professed belief and her behaviour. Standardly, these tensions are attributed to the person's awareness of the truth (Deweese-Boyd, 2021: §3.1) and the cognitive dissonance is thought to be caused by the clash between her evidence and her desire for Arnold not to be having an affair (Scott-Kakures, 2021: 472–473).

In my view, rather than immediately assuming that they know the truth while being self-deceived or that they detect an inconsistency between their desires and evidence, we can explain the tension or the dissonance by saying that Sid and Maria think that this is not the conclusion they would normally draw. Maria might think to herself 'Perhaps, they are right. Would I think the same if this was Sharon's husband? (Who acts suspiciously, by the way)'. The self-deceiver's realisation that she is deviating from her own normal behaviour does not entail that she also knows the truth, but it does suggest that she senses that something is off, which easily explains the symptoms often ascribed to self-deceivers.

Allow me to outline the vital step in my analysis of the suspected self-deceivers' behaviour one more time. The analogy with other-deception is in the following: the predator female is not being herself because being herself does not bring her food (i.e., generate the result), the job candidate is not being themself because this will not get them a job, and Maria is not being herself because being herself will not satisfy her desire that Arnold is not having an affair. The behaviour or the trait the predator firefly, the job candidate, and Maria employ must be of the kind whose function is to mislead – even if they do not realise that it misleads. Therefore, as long as we have reasons to think that Maria is not being herself, we can say that she is a self-deceiver even if we cannot determine whether Arnold is having an affair, which is a very neat result. Another neat result is that if her behaviour also misleads some of her friends, she would count as deceiving them just as weak crayfish may mislead both their opponents and themselves with the same trait. The final benefit is that the behavioural tension and doxastic discomfort are easily explained without the need to appeal to rather serious divisions in the mind.

That said, I am denying neither that some self-deceivers do (intermittently) know the truth 'deep down' nor that some people deceive themselves intentionally. These situations are not inconsistent with my functional view; however, because they are rather controversial, these cases need to be analysed individually and not as a part of a general theory of self-deception. I already argued that some of these situations involve bald-faced lying to oneself (Krstić, 2023a), they may also involve repression or wilful ignorance (Lynch, 2016), conflicting beliefs could be located in different context-dependent belief-corpora (Egan, 2008; Quilty-Dunn and Mandelbaum, 2018; Bendaña and Mandelbaum, 2021), or it could be that the person's credence shifts depending on the context (Chan and Rowbottom, 2019).

Recently, Curzer (2024b: 5) argued that interpretations that do not appeal to subsystems fail to capture the phenomenology of this kind of self-deception. The problem with this move is that (contra Curzer) this phenomenology is not directly observable in the phenomenon itself but is rather a theoretical postulate. For example, Curzer (2024b: 6) writes that most cases of this kind of self-deception involve 'first-order rather than second-order beliefs', but we obviously cannot observe the difference between the two kinds of beliefs in others. We can only *infer it* from the person's behaviour and our preferred theories, which is what Curzer does: he (2024b: 7) writes that the person's behaviour is 'indicating that he does not just exchange one belief for the other, but rather retains both beliefs throughout'. This is not a direct observation but an explanation derived from a specific theory. Therefore, the 'data' Curzer is talking about is not evidence that the theory is correct since the theory itself is used to interpret the data. We cannot identify or observe conflicting beliefs, even less agent-like subsystems, in a person. We can only posit them using our preferred theoretical framework in order to explain phenomena as how they present themselves *to us*.

The general theory that I am offering gives us a framework for determining whether cases in which *it seems to us* that the person knows the truth 'deep down' indeed involve self-deception, and this framework is grounded in a refined conceptual analysis of deception. The word 'refined' is important. The need to posit conflicting beliefs is a direct consequence of a *flawed* conceptual analysis of interpersonal deception; it is not something we can directly and pretheoretically observe in self-deception. This is not to say that no self-deceiver has ever believed that p and that not p, but rather that, in most cases discussed in the literature, we do not have strong evidence to support this claim. A further case-by-case analysis is required.

4 The Not-So-Beneficial Result of Self-Deception

4.1 Introduction

Philosophers predominantly think that deception systematically benefits the deceiver. This need not come at any tangible cost for the victim and may, in addition to the benefit, also bring some costs to the deceiver. People often lie in order to save themselves from embarrassment, disapproval, or having their feelings hurt (DePaulo, 2019: 440). In these cases, the deceiver's benefit is psychological, and the dupe suffers only epistemic harm. Also, some people lie to their doctors about their diet, about how much they exercise or drink, or say that they do not smoke (Fallis, 2015a: 413). This behaviour tends to lead to incorrect and ineffective treatments, which may harm the deceiver – who is quite often aware of this consequence. Nonetheless, the deceiver still receives some benefit: the reason to engage in deception is 'saving face', and the harm is the price to be paid for this benefit to be received.

Self-deception is predominantly understood as generating a result very similar to that played by these double-edged deceptive lies. Therefore, the received literature predominantly focuses on cases in which the person ends up believing a proposition she wants to be true. These would be cases of a person deceiving themselves into thinking that their partner is not having an affair, or of parents deceiving themselves into thinking that their child is not abusing drugs, or of a man deceiving himself into thinking that he is not losing hair, that his memory is as good as it was, that he is smarter than he is, a better driver, and so on. The deceiver's benefit here is a (temporary) psychological relief at their epistemic and practical expense (a false belief will guide their behaviour), which makes self-deception a reality-coping mechanism.

Some philosophers (e.g., Van Leeuwen, 2007a: 423) call this phenomenon *wishful self-deception,* and in cases in which self-deception is continuous with wishful thinking, this name correctly describes the phenomenon. However, some self-deceivers do not really want a specific proposition to be true (due to its unwelcome corollaries) but, nevertheless, welcome it in a sense in which the lesser of two evils is welcome. Maria, for instance, could make herself believe that she could not care less that Arnold is having an affair, a proposition she does not really want to be true (she does not want Arnold to be having an affair) but, nonetheless, welcomes in this situation – as a stress-relief. Similarly, some parents might admit that their child is smoking pot but deceive themselves into thinking that this is just an occasional joint. The man could deceive himself into believing that he does not care that he is losing his hair or that his age significantly affects his memory while admitting that these things are indeed happening to him. Therefore, *welcome self-deception* seems like a better name.

Some self-deceivers, however, seem to cause themselves to believe something they would prefer not to be true and would not welcome in any sense or scenario. These would be cases of parents who deceived themselves into believing that they are to blame for their child's death, although the child died of leukaemia, of a spouse who deceived themself into believing that their beloved partner is unfaithful, of an adolescent who deceived themself into believing that they are overweight, of a bright young college student who deceived themself into believing that they are less able than they are, of a professor who deceived themself into believing that they are passing themself off as much more capable than they really are (the imposter syndrome), and so on.

Van Leeuwen (2007a, 2007b) calls this self-deception *dreadful* since some people end up believing their worst fears. Nevertheless, others simply end up believing a proposition they do not appear to welcome: as in making yourself believe that you will embarrass yourself at the upcoming trivia pub quiz, that you look silly in this hat, and someone will think that their gaining weight or losing hair is an inconvenience rather than a dreaded possibility. Funkhouser (2019) calls this self-deception *negative* as opposed to *positive* since the person has a negative attitude towards their self-deceptive belief. This name may also be a bit too strong: it suggests that there is something good about positive self-deception and bad about negative self-deception, which is likely not the case and, in fact, on some views, people benefit from their 'negative' beliefs. Mele (e.g., 1999, 2001) calls this self-deception *twisted* as opposed to *straight*. This terminology is consistent with the standard view that people engage in self-deception for some benefit. However, I will argue that this kind of self-deception is not a deviation from the rule, since there is no 'rule', which makes 'twisted' a misleading name. Therefore, I prefer *unwelcome* self-deception (following Barnes, 1997; Scott-Kakures, 2000). Finally, I will argue that self-deception is sometimes *non-welcome*. Some people neither welcome nor unwelcome the product of their self-deception, and their self-deceptive response could be strategic.

Let us now see why unwelcome self-deception is problematic by considering a case that I developed by combining Zelda Fitzgerald's documented jealousy with an anonymous confession I found online (modified from Krstić, 2021: 847–848).[4]

> *Zelda* confidently believes that she possesses plenty of evidence that her husband Scott is having an affair with his new close friend Ernest. Although Scott denies vigorously that they are having an affair, they are getting along great, and that can't be right – she is quite sure of that. In fact, the more she thinks about it, the more evidence she finds. Thinking about that one time they were in Paris and met Ernest, she remembered how Scott went to the bathroom in the middle of the night, and then she became convinced that he actually went to see Ernest. Cheating fits Scott, she reasons, precisely because he's such an unlikely person to do it, and their marriage has been falling apart for months now. Zelda does not exhibit any signs of delusion or schizophrenia. Therefore, she is not pathologically paranoid, but she does seem to be deceiving herself: she has absolutely no real evidence of the affair, and she does not seem to be her normal self. Had it been someone else's husband, she would not have made these ridiculous accusations. The worst thing is that she certainly wants neither Scott to be having an affair nor that she believes that; her belief is making her desperate.

Zelda causes herself to believe that Scott is having an affair with Ernest even though this belief not only makes her miserable but is also obviously epistemically unjustified. Her case is philosophically important because its result is a conclusion that the person should naturally avoid making both for strong psychological and epistemic reasons. Zelda keeps coming up with reasons in support of her unjustified belief while actively wanting to believe the exact opposite. What can she possibly gain from causing herself to believe this? The most obvious benefit I can get by harming myself epistemically and practically is giving myself some psychological relief, but Zelda gains no relief; her behaviour only generates anxiety.

The case sits uneasily with many influential accounts. For example, Robert Trivers (Trivers, 2011; von Hippel and Trivers, 2011) argues that self-deception evolved to facilitate interpersonal deception by allowing people to avoid cues that might reveal their deceptive intent. This hypothesis may explain cases like the self-deceived weak crayfish, but it makes little sense when applied to *Zelda*. Why should Zelda want to make other people believe this proposition? She is probably ashamed of this, and she might be desperately trying to keep the affair a secret. Cases like *Zelda* pose a problem for the idea that what explains why organisms engage in self-deception is the fact that it systematically generates some benefit for them.

---

[4] The confession: https://askthepsych.com/atp/2010/04/29/delusional-jealousy-husband-wrongfully-suspects-me-of-cheating/#google_vignette.

Even though my functional view is consistent with the existence of altruistic deception, it may seem that because I distinguish the result from the function of deceptive traits or behaviours and I say that the result explains *why* people engage in self-deception, these cases are a problem for my view as well. This assumption is incorrect. The functional view neither assumes that self-deception is an adaptive mechanism (§3.2.1) nor that we can explain the origin of self-deception with a single hypothesis, namely by saying that it evolved because it aids anxiety reduction, facilitating other-deception, and so on. Rather, because it assumes that self-deception – just like any deception – is a heterogeneous phenomenon and that different organisms engage in it for different reasons, my view can leave this question open (similarly, Funkhouser, 2017, 2019: §7). In this section, I discuss this idea in more detail and highlight its advantages. This hypothesis is the final piece in my view.

I first present some attempts to reconcile the idea that self-deception brings some benefit to the agent with the existence of unwelcome self-deception and resolve some concerns (§4.2). I then (§4.3) introduce altruistic, benevolent, self-punishing, or polyvalent self-deception and argue that the agent's benefit cannot explain why people deceive themselves in these cases. Finally, in some cases, the result of self-deception does not explain why the person engages in it at all – the product is neither welcome nor unwelcome. Therefore, the best we can do is to conduct a case-by-case analysis of self-deception, and the functional view gives us this opportunity at no cost.

I will not talk in terms of the self-deceiver's motive to make themself believe a particular proposition. Generating a specific result (anxiety reduction, vigilance, etc.) may explain why we have self-deception in this particular case, even when this is not introspectively accessible to the self-deceiver and even if the self-deceiver, such as Zelda, is motivated to cause herself to believe a different proposition. As said, the relevant self-deceptive behaviour/trait could be an automatic, pre-conscious, strategic response to a specific stimulus that is analogous to how a firefly responds to a specific signal and can be described by the 'If in context C, perform behaviour φ / activate trait Φ' conditional (§4.2.2). So, let us see how the received views try to deal with unwelcome self-deception.

4.2 Unwelcome Self-Deception

4.2.1 The Received Views

The problem unwelcome self-deception poses for the standard view is twofold: not only that the view needs to identify the benefit people systematically get by making themselves believe something they do not want to be true, this benefit needs to be consistent with the benefit people systematically get from believing what they want to be true. One solution is that engaging in self-deception (welcome and unwelcome) is set off by the need to reduce anxiety (Johnston, 1988; Barnes, 1997). Barnes argues that, while welcome self-deception reduces anxiety with respect to the acquired belief, deceiving oneself into believing something one does not welcome reduces anxiety associated with some other proposition. The following case should illustrate her point.

> *John's* friend George agrees to do something when asked by John's wife, Mary, but had refused to do it when asked by John. John, who cares about George's regard, is taken aback by George's refusal of his request, and he begins to suspect and, ultimately, believe that George and Mary are having an affair. John, by self-deceptively believing that his wife has been unfaithful avoids concluding, as he otherwise might have concluded, that George's reaction is a consequence of his having higher regard for Mary than for John. (Barnes, 1997: 41).

Barnes's explanation is that, by misinterpreting evidence, John trades higher anxiety, which is caused by believing the proposition supported by George's behaviour, for lesser anxiety, caused by acquiring the self-deceptive belief. The more powerful desire causes John to deceive himself. However, believing the unwelcome proposition would reduce anxiety only if John cared more about George's regard than Mary's fidelity, which is unlikely. The belief that his wife is unfaithful actually increases John's anxiety (Scott-Kakures, 2001: 321). And the hypothesis deals even worse with *Zelda* because her anxiety is generated exclusively by her self-deception. Therefore, reducing anxiety seems to be an unlikely general cause of self-deception.

Because unwelcome self-deception often causes or increases anxiety, some scholars suggest that what explains its existence is that it brings practical benefit at the cost of inflicting some typically short-term (side-effect) harm, such as increased anxiety, when the benefit outweighs the harm. The basis for this view was provided by Mele (1999: 122, 2001: §V, 2006: 114), who writes that, whereas for many people it is more important to avoid acquiring the false belief that their spouses are having affairs, the converse may well be true of some insecure, jealous people. Mele's proposal is very convincing and influential, and it comes in many variations. This version is based on two theses.

The first is taken from Sharpsteen and Kirkpatrick (1997: 627), who write that the jealousy complex is a mechanism for maintaining close relationships that appears to be 'triggered by separation, or the threat of separation, from attachment figures'. Let this be the *threat thesis*. The second is the thesis that the concern for minimising having costly false beliefs drives lay hypothesis testing, the so-called FTL theory. Recall, according to FTL (§3.1), the greater the predicted damage caused by falsely accepting that p, the greater the cost of falsely accepting it and, as a result, the greater the aversion towards falsely believing it. And the level of aversion towards falsely believing a proposition determines the threshold for accepting or rejecting it: the lower the threshold, the less evidence is sufficient for accepting a proposition, and the threshold is low if the expected cost of believing it falsely is low (Mele, 1999, 2001, 2006; see, Scott-Kakures, 2000).

On this view, Zelda's strong, jealous desire to maintain her relationship with Scott plays a role in rendering the false belief that Scott is *not* having an affair a 'costly' error. Since believing erroneously that Scott is not having an affair may cause her not to take steps to protect the relationship against an intruder, Zelda would have a higher aversion towards falsely believing this proposition than towards falsely believing the one that causes her suffering (Mele, 2001: §5, 2006: 114; Lauria, Preissmann, and Clément, 2016: 127, n. 10; Gadsby, 2022: 252). Therefore, she deceives herself because this will cause herself to take steps to protect her relationship (her benefit), and this is more important than the harm she will also bring about.

This proposal can even explain the fact that, by being unreasonably jealous, the self-deceiver may jeopardise or harm her marriage. Recall, self-deceivers are acting according to their *perceived* (rather than real) primary error (Friedrich, 1993; see, Scott-Kakures, 2000) and what this error is in any particular case depends upon a person's current motivational, affective, and attentional condition. Because costs are subjective, accepting the 'affair' hypothesis need not be a costly error from the self-deceiver's perspective. We should also expect some degree of myopia in these cases that will affect the cost-benefit assessment: Zelda and John seem to be discounting the possibility of paying some distant costs, such as harming their relationships with their jealousy.

One concern is that the *threat thesis* limits the application of the view only to cases of unwelcome self-deception that involve jealousy (Lazar, 1999: 275), but this concern can be resolved. The self-deceiver need not be jealous; something else could be under threat. For instance, a view of oneself as being the sort of person who would never be taken unawares by a cheating spouse or of oneself as being very attractive or highly regarded by everyone could be under threat. Nonetheless, one problem remains: Where did Zelda get the idea that she could be taken unawares by her cheating spouse or that Scott thinks that she is not attractive?

One of the main ideas of this proposal is that the function of believing that Scott is having an affair is to help Zelda protect the relationship against the intruder; however, there is no threat of separation that could trigger jealousy, suspicion, or this kind of evidence assessment. In fact, it is the other way around: the way she assesses evidence and her distrust cause Zelda to think that there is a threat of separation. Zelda invents evidence, and she interprets counterevidence to p as evidence that p: she thinks that cheating fits Scott because he is such an unlikely person to do it. Thus, while it may be correct that Zelda's jealousy (distrust) makes the 'no-affair' hypothesis a costly error, Mele's theory cannot tell us where the threat came from. Scott's behaviour involves nothing extraordinary, nothing that should cause her to think that she is not very attractive or that she should not trust him. The jealousy/distrust/etc. makes the 'no-affair' hypothesis a costly error. This explanation, thus, raises two concerns: first, it understands the aetiology of unwelcome self-deception backwards and, second, it cannot tell us what triggers self-deception in people like Zelda.

One may object that Zelda is not inventing evidence but rather merely interpreting a fact (the absence of evidence for p), or even evidence in favour of not-p, as evidence for p. Perhaps, there is a sense in which Zelda does not invent evidence when she analyses Scott's going to the bathroom but rather puts enormous weight on what is really very weak evidence. However, this still raises the first concern: it is the jealousy (distrust, protecting self-esteem, etc.) that explains Zelda's way of interpreting the evidence, not the other way around. Given the prior probability and the likelihood, the formation of the thought 'Scott went to see Ernest when he was in the bathroom' involves a very large deviation from the normal Bayesian updating. Therefore, to handle the case, the FTL view requires Zelda to have an unreasonably low threshold for what counts as evidence in support of the 'affair' proposition if her accepting this proposition is to generate jealousy, suspicion, or threaten Zelda's self-image or self-respect. However, as a consequence, the first factor (jealousy, distrust, self-image) becomes redundant in the aetiology of self-deception: it cannot tell us *why* Zelda deceives herself.

Inventing evidence is an important feature of some cases of self-deception that cannot be explained solely by appealing to Mele's two theses. Recall the case of parents who deceived themselves into believing that they were to be blamed for the death of their child who died of leukaemia – call it *Heartbroken Parents*. No information could function as evidence in support of their belief. There must be something in the parents' or Zelda's psychology that overrides their normal hypothesis-testing mechanisms, but the *threat thesis* cannot tell us what.

It could be that it is not the job of Mele's theory to tell us where Zelda's threat came from; this is part of the backstory rather than the theory. Maybe Zelda is standardly jealous or distrustful because she was badly hurt by the affairs of her previous partners. This backstory, then, easily explains Zelda's inventing evidence: the pre-existing jealousy affects the Bayesian updating by making the 'affair' hypothesis more probable than it is. This is a sensible idea, but it does not explain *all* cases of unwelcome self-deception. I do not see how one could sensibly fill in the details of *Heartbroken Parents* to make it consistent with the FTL. What kind of an event could make the hypothesis 'We are not responsible for our child's death' a more costly error?

All variations of the Melean view raise similar concerns. Scott-Kakures (2001, see 2000), for example, suggests that self-deception makes the agent's goals and interests, such as avoiding danger, more likely to be fulfilled than not. The modification of the Melean view is in that the costly error is not measured with respect to falsely accepting/rejecting that p but rather with respect to the agent's focal goals and interests, which may be promoted even by falsely believing/rejecting that p. A true belief may sometimes be a costly error, as in the case in which there is a danger of your partner having an affair and making you believe that the partner is having an affair will help you to prevent this from happening. On this view, that is, by acquiring the unwelcome belief, self-deceivers make sure that they will take all necessary steps to avoid the unwelcome state of affairs (see, Funkhouser, 2019: 235).

A similar hypothesis elegantly explains many cases of the self-deceptive imposter syndrome, a false, unjustified belief that one is successful in a highly competitive job due to luck. The explanation is that, because they believe that they lack the relevant ability but that hard work can compensate for this shortcoming, people with this syndrome work harder and thus perform better. Their negative appraisal of their own qualities provides additional motivation by signalling the need for more effort, and this additional motivation is both advantageous in the relevant context and outweighs the relevant affective disutility (Gadsby, 2022).

Notwithstanding its merits, this view does raise some concerns if we try to use it as a general account of the origin of self-deception. Say that an athlete systematically deceives herself into believing that she is injured before important competitions – call this *Hurt Athlete*. Acquiring this belief systematically undermines her performance or even prevents her from competing rather than serving her best interests. Appealing to her perceived primary error requires explaining why the perceived error would be to believe that she is hurt. If the competition is important enough, many athletes compete even while hurt (often under severe painkillers), thereby risking serious injuries. In this case, the utility of the false belief not only does not outweigh the disutility of the true belief, but it only generates disutility.

We could say *Zelda*, *John*, and *Heartbroken Parents* involve a malfunctioned self-protective mechanism, an adaptive disposition that occasionally backfires. However, this position begs the question – it takes it as true that self-deception is a self-protective mechanism, which is exactly what is at stake here – and cannot explain *Hurt Athlete* since she harms herself systematically. Nevertheless, some cases seem to fit this hypothesis. Consider *Barbara*.

> *Barbara*, a busy young attorney, leaves home on her daily commute, late for an important meeting. As she nears the freeway entrance, she is suddenly taken with worry that she has left her gas stove on. Barbara does not remember whether she had left it on. Due to a disagreement she had with her husband, she was absent-minded that day, which could have distracted her from her routine. She desperately tries to visualize turning off the burner, but she cannot. And then her fear of her house burning down becomes so real that it causes her to believe that she did leave it on. Convinced now that she has left the stove burning, she calls her husband but he has already left home. At great inconvenience, she returns home only to discover that the burner is off. (Scott-Kakures, 2001: 314).

The unwelcome belief increases Barbara's chances of preserving her house. If Barbara falsely believes that she has left the stove on, the cost is relatively low (she will return only to find that all is well) but, if Barbara falsely believes that she has not left the stove on, the cost is extremely high – her house might burn down (Scott-Kakures, 2001: 323). Therefore, this mechanism obviously serves her goals and interests, and there is no need to think that Barbara's psychology makes her in any way more prone to self-deception than other people, which is a concomitant of Mele's proposal, for instance.

However, why think that Barbara's behaviour involves self-deception? After all, she cannot remember turning the stove off and she was absent-minded that day. Her belief, though false, is neither epistemically unjustified nor irrational, and the function of her behaviour is not to mislead. Levy (2016) gives us three possible interpretations of this behaviour. According to the first, Barbara's thought would not be a belief but rather a default thought, a subpersonally generated simulation similar to imagination (Gerrans, 2014). The default network is a mechanism of testing thoughts for consistency and adequacy, which in turn may qualify them for representational states such as beliefs. When unsupervised, default thoughts may occupy the role of representational states and make people act on them: people may think that they believe that they have left the stove on and go back to turn it off. Default thoughts may equally become beliefs if the mind judges that the thought is reasonable, which would be the second interpretation of the case. Accordingly, it could be that Barbara's fear triggers the relevant default thought, 'My house may burn down', which, being judged as reasonable according to prior beliefs and available evidence, gets passed as correct and adopted as a belief. Finally, it could be that the fear is caused by Barbara's representation of the stove as on; this fear generates anxiety, which then directly influences her behaviour. Each of these explanations is more plausible than the one that says that Barbara deceived herself into believing that she left the stove on.

Nelkin (2002) and Funkhouser (2005) argue that both welcome and unwelcome self-deceivers want to believe the proposition they end up with. Welcome self-deceivers want this proposition to reflect the state of affairs, while unwelcome self-deceivers want their belief to aid in preventing this state of affairs from occurring. Unwelcome self-deceivers, thus, want to believe the unwelcome proposition or, at least, to have some first-person qualities associated with such a belief, but they do *not* want that what they believe is true. Being the jealous, insecure type, Zelda wants that Scott is not having an affair and, out of caution, wants to believe that Scott is having an affair (Funkhouser, 2005: 298) – since believing what she does not want to be true will make her more vigilant. However, postulating this kind of motivation is theoretically problematic, and the function of this motivation is unclear. Zelda and Barbara can perform all cautionary actions even without believing the unwelcome proposition (McKay and Dennett, 2009: 500–501). Therefore, it does not make sense for them to want to believe it and cause themselves unnecessary stress.

Perhaps the right kind of protective mechanism should be based on the wish to believe that one is at risk of getting cancer (losing one's job, failing the exam) or, analogously, that one is at risk of losing her husband's affection. This modification may explain some variations of *Zelda* and *John*, but it is still too narrow. Take, for example, *Hurt Athlete*. Believing that she is at risk of getting hurt right before the big competition will reduce her chances of success, which systematically defeats the purpose of the supposed protective mechanism. Why would this athlete want to believe that she is hurt? It makes more sense for her to cause herself to believe that she is not as good as she is, which might prompt her to train harder (Funkhouser, 2017: 237, n. 24; Gadsby, 2022) or to lower her expectations (Funkhouser, 2019: 236). Finally, the Nelkin–Funkhouser hypothesis cannot explain the behaviour of the parents who blame themselves for their child's death. The unwelcome belief will not help them to take all necessary steps to avoid the unwelcome state of affairs.

The only cases in which believing what one does not want to be the case but in which the belief is systematically serving the person's interests are *Barbara* and some involving the imposter syndrome. However, because *Barbara* does not involve self-deception, all we are left with are some cases of the imposter syndrome, which suggests that furthering the self-deceiver's interests in this way is more an exception to a systematic practice rather than a sign of a systematic practice.

The final explanation says that the self-deceiver's emotional state primes relevant processing systems to gather evidence in a biased fashion, which – depending on the state – sometimes produces welcome and sometimes unwelcome beliefs. The welcome self-deceiver cannot face some unwelcome reality and so she turns her head away, whereas the unwelcome self-deceiver cannot stop thinking about some unwelcome reality and so she treats some data as evidence that what she fears of is true (similarly Lazar, 1999; Bach, 2009; Galeotti, 2018: 52–55). In unwelcome believing, the person's anxious emotion makes her incapable of getting her mind off the subject. She, therefore, dismisses information she can easily put out of her mind and concentrates on information she cannot put out of her mind, which makes the dreadful possibility more realistic than it really is. However, because the function of these mechanisms is not to mislead, this proposal cannot be used in an analysis of self-deception. Also, the priming mechanism does not apply to non-welcome self-deception (§4.3) since these self-deceivers are emotionally neutral, I am not sure how it could apply to *Heartbroken* Parents, and it sits uneasily with cases in which self-deceivers consistently probe the unwelcome hypothesis (Scott-Kakures, 2000: e.g., 361–362).

In conclusion, the idea that self-deception systematically brings people some benefit is rather problematic. However, before abandoning it, I will first try to refine it.

4.2.2 A Possible Refinement

All the solutions discussed thus far say that people deceive themselves because they somehow benefit from this. They only differ in what kind of benefit the person receives. So, perhaps we could simply say that people engage in self-deception because it benefits them in some sense, period. And here is one way in which this proposal can be cashed out as a systematic theory.

At least three factors determine why people engage in self-deception in some contexts but not in others and in a specific direction (welcome, unwelcome). The first is how the person perceives herself, namely, in a positive or negative light. The second factor is how she assesses the relevant context and what is at stake in it: low stakes mean low motivation, and low motivation means low probability of self-deception. And the third is how the utility of the relevant beliefs figures in relation to (1) and (2); namely, what is the perceived utility of the belief in the relevant context. I will address these each of factors in turn, but briefly – since they have already been widely discussed.[5]

---

[5] I would recommend reading Funkhouser's (2017: 234–239, 2019: §7) cost-benefit analysis of self-deception and Gadsby's (2022) analysis of the imposter syndrome, noting that my analysis was developed independently of theirs and cannot be reduced to either of them.

Some studies suggest that most people have unrealistically positive views of themselves and that they hold unrealistic optimism about the future (Taylor and Brown, 1988; Taylor et al., 1989; Trivers, 2011: 15–18). For instance, most people think that they are in more control of their life than they in fact are and they take more credit for success while denying responsibility for failure (Langer and Rodin, 1976; Snyder et al., 1992; Kenny and Kashy, 1994). This bias is unconscious (Epley and Whitchurch, 2008), but it is not always inflationary. People with negative self-views preferentially seek negative self-evaluations, and some of them even divorce spouses who perceive them in an overly positive manner (Swann, 1983).

This discrepancy in self-evaluations explains why some people cause themselves to falsely believe that they are not losing hair and some that they are overweight or that they lack some important abilities, but it is insufficient for a general account: these self-evaluative biases are not hallmarks of certain types of personality. Therefore, even though some people may be more prone to self-deception than others, we should not think that there is something like a self-deception-prone type of personality. In different contexts and with different things at stake, the same person may exhibit different biases or exhibit no biases whatsoever. A man may absolutely dread losing his hair as an adolescent and merely find it unwelcome later in his life, since he no longer thinks that losing hair will affect his social status. Also, consider the results of a study conducted by John and Robins (1994). Their participants were MBA students at the University of California, Berkeley, who were simulating the meeting of a compensation committee in a large company. Some 35 per cent of the participants showed a self-enhancement bias (positively inflating one's self-understanding), 15 per cent exhibited a self-diminishment bias, while the remaining 50 per cent were rather accurate. I think that the fact that half of the participants did not exhibit any bias makes sense on the thesis that performing better or worse than others had no motivational effect on them. A likely explanation is that they did not see this as a competition but rather as a task calling for teamwork. This study, then, suggests that the direction of the bias depends not only on one's personality but also on what one takes to be at stake in that context. This is why the second factor is rather important.

The third factor explains how self-deceptive belief figures in the 'why X deceived themselves in this particular way in context C' equation. For example, in some instances of the imposter syndrome, 'the domain is one where the individual believes that effort can substitute ability, such that a belief that one lacks ability will have a motivating (rather than demotivating) effect' (Gadsby, 2022: 253). So, the utility of the relevant belief is in that it provides a beneficial additional motivational boost for the agent that will increase their chances of success. This explains the behaviour of those people who negatively see some of their abilities relative to some domains of their life in certain contexts but, in general, have positive self-views. Some people, however, have negative self-views and they preferentially seek negative self-evaluations. These people, then, with respect to the same domains of their life and the same contexts, may just need reasons to allow themselves to fail, a reason that will excuse their lack of trying, which counts as having utility for them. And this may happen even to people with positive self-views when the cost of additional effort may be a price too high to pay. If I need to invest significant resources to obtain X in C and the probability of obtaining X in C is insufficiently high considering the cost, deceiving myself into believing that the probability is substantially lower than it actually is would allow me to abstain from trying to get X in C and thereby preserve my resources for some future endeavour or maintain my overall wellbeing (which would be significantly affected by my failure).

This short exposition yields the following explanatory framework: (i) people engage in self-deception to secure their focal benefit (universal kind of result) and what determines whether this benefit will be secured by acquiring a welcome or unwelcome belief is (ii) how the person perceives herself and the relevant context (i.e., what is at stake), and (iii) which belief generates greater perceived utility – relative to (i) and (ii). Notice, one's *perspective* on the issue – condition (ii) – is vital in this equation since it determines both whether the person will engage in self-deception or not and whether the product of self-deception will be welcome or unwelcome. Let us now apply this framework, call it *refined self-interest view*, to the cases discussed.

Zelda and Scott's marriage is going through a difficult phase: the 'affair' hypothesis explains Zelda's marital problems while shifting blame to Scott, thereby protecting Zelda's positive self-image; this is the utility of the self-deceptive belief. But it could also be that Zelda is avoiding the thought that the marriage is going through a difficult phase because Scott does not find her sexually attractive. As a result, 'Cheating fits Scott' means that his faulty character rather than her lack of attractiveness caused their marital problems. In both variations, what explains why she engages in self-deception (condition 1 of my functional analysis of self-deception) is her need to protect her positive self-image (focal benefit) in this context and the fact that this need outweighs the cost of suffering some harm. Her behaviour is not so strange after all.

Hurt Athlete is best explained along the lines of Quattrone and Tversky's (1984) analysis of self-handicapping strategies. People engage in self-handicapping strategies in order to ascribe the failure to their handicap and not to their lack of ability to succeed: 'by drinking or taking drugs [before the upcoming IQ test], any level of intellectual performance would not destroy the belief that one is basically bright, for even failure could be attributed to the debilitating effects of alcohol' (Quattrone and Tversky, 1984: 248). The need to avoid explaining the failure to one's lack of ability to succeed, that is, explains why one engages in self-deception just as the need to deter predators explains why the snake plays dead. The athlete's belief that she is hurt protects her positive self-image by giving her a reason not to compete or an excuse if she fails to meet her expectations at the competition, which explains why she systematically deceives herself.

Funkhouser and Hallam (2024: §3.3) argue that self-handicapping strategies require elaborate unconscious knowledge and an unconscious 'plan' to create an excuse for an anticipated failure or suboptimal performance. On their view, then, these cases of self-deception require a deeply divided mind and a kind of intention to mislead oneself. Allow me to briefly suggest a simpler solution that does not require positing subconscious deceptive intentions. This behaviour could predominantly be an automatic, pre-conscious strategic response to a specific stimulus analogous to a firefly's response to a specific signal (condition 1 of my analysis). Relative to the three factors I discussed, some athletes systematically encourage themselves before the competitions, whereas some systematically come up with excuses. Rather than unconsciously evaluating the evidence, context, the probability of failure, and the plausibility of the excuse, these self-deceivers, just like their non-self-deceiving peers, may simply react strategically: in context C, they perform behaviour φ where, for some athletes, φ-ing is encouraging oneself, and for some others, it is coming up with excuses. This is another example of how the fact that it can easily explain how people strategically and without a plan deceive themselves is an important advantage of the functional view.

The case of the man who thinks that the government is spying on him can be explained along the lines of Bentall's (1994: 353) thesis that persecutory delusions protect the individual against chronic feelings of low self-esteem. This man thinks that he is important enough for the government to see him as a threat. The paranoia gives him a sense of value and feeds his self-regard (condition 1), thereby securing his focal benefit, which explains why he deceives himself.

The proposed account seems rather successful: while we have identified one general reason to engage in self-deception, we can apply a case-by-case analysis of the phenomenon by reasonably filling in some details. However, this is still not good enough: while this hypothesis explains many or most cases of self-deception, it cannot be a general analysis of self-deception. Some cases of self-deception are non-welcome (so, the belief's utility plays no role in its aetiology), and a non-negligible class of self-deceptive behaviour systematically does not benefit the agents in any sense.

4.3 No Benefit for the Deceiver

Human altruistic deception is performed for someone else's benefit at the deceiver's expense (DePaulo et al., 1996: esp. 983; Gneezy, 2005; Erat and Gneezy, 2012). Altruistic deceivers, however, need not pay a high cost. Thirty-three per cent of participants of Erat and Gneezy's (2012: 725) study based on sender-receiver games were willing to transmit misinformation that would bring $10 to the receiver at the expense of not getting a dollar themselves. From the existence of human altruistic deception, I infer the existence of *altruistic self-deception* (Krstić, 2021). One such case is when Maria cannot accept the truth because the truth is inconsistent with her perception of Arnold as having good moral character. Accordingly, what explains why she engages in self-deception (i.e., the 'result') is Arnold's benefit. A more altruistic case would involve deception not to preserve *her* image of him but to avoid a confrontation that Arnold would find painful. If, that is, Maria 'φ-s in context C due to an influence of a desire, emotion, or interest' (condition 1), it is because of the desire not to cause any inconvenience to Arnold. In *The Hangover* (Warner Bros., 2009), for instance, 'Stu' Price keeps finding excuses for the behaviour of his abusive, bossy, and cheating girlfriend, Mellissa. Stu does this to avoid causing inconvenience to Melissa and at his own expense.

The hypothesis that some cases of self-deception are caused by desires to generate altruistic results (my condition 1) easily explains why a parent who deceived herself into believing that her child's chances of recovery are good may allow herself to undergo a painful or possibly fatal medical procedure to save her child. In such cases, the self-deceiver's benefit – for example, anxiety reduction – seems to be a side-effect rather than the reason for engaging in self-deception. There is an element of kin selection here, of course, but we cannot generalise this to all similar cases. People regularly sacrifice themselves for strangers or ideals.

The refined self-interest view cannot explain deceiving oneself for genuinely altruistic motives. In contrast, because it models self-deception on interpersonal deception and because it does not require the deceiver to benefit from deception, the functional analysis can easily explain deceiving oneself not only for altruistic but equally for any other reasons. Let us consider some cases.

Some people deceive others to punish themselves. One famous example is the notorious 'suicide by cop' in which a suicidal person forces the police to use deadly force. From the existence of self-punishing interpersonal deception, I infer the existence of *self-punishing self-deception*. Self-punishment perfectly well explains why the *Heartbroken Parents* engage in self-deception: even if some self-punishers find some psychological pleasure in their punishment, it seems unlikely that these parents find pleasure in their suffering and it is even unlikelier that this pleasure *explains why* they engage in self-deception in the sense in which the blood circulation explains why the heart beats. Rather, they seem to be punishing themselves because they need to increase the intensity of their suffering and give their child the kind of grieving they think it deserves. So, the desire that explains why they engage in self-deception is the (unconscious) desire to harm themselves and this desire is easily captured by condition 1 of the functional view but not by the refined self-interest analysis.

Benevolent deception, which generates benefit for someone else at no cost to the deceiver, is also very common. Erat and Gneezy (2012) give many examples of the so-called white lies, lies told to help others and, in the study conducted by DePaulo et al. (1996: 991–992), one out of every four lies their participants told were to benefit other people and, when only women were involved, this ratio went up to 50 per cent. Some examples of pro-social and white lies are when a supervisor avoids giving fully honest feedback to her poorly performing employee in order to avoid reducing their confidence and future performance, or when we tell our friends or even strangers that they look lovely when they actually do not, and so on (Dietz, 2019).

From the existence of benevolent interpersonal deception, I infer the existence of *benevolent self-deception* (Krstić, 2021). Benevolent self-deceivers mainly protect an idealised picture of their close relatives or their nation, religion, team members, and so on. For example, some people seem to be deceiving themselves into thinking that their team is much better than it really is, that their nation originates from Alexander the Great, that their race is superior to other races, that the Arch of Covenant is buried in their country, and so forth. Many, if not most, cases of benevolent and altruistic self-deception could be explained as reciprocal altruism or benevolence that, ultimately, benefits the self-deceiver (Trivers, 2011: 19–20, 63–64; Funkhouser, 2019: §7.3), in which case the refined self-interest analysis applies, but not all of them. Consider a Christian monk who sees all and only good in every person. Say that this monk acquires and maintains some of his beliefs regarding other people's moral qualities (e.g., he exaggerates their positive nature) in a way that counts as involving self-deception. What explains this behaviour is the monk's love towards humanity; this is the interest that causes him to φ (the result from condition 1), and this interest is purely benevolent. The functional analysis easily explains this case but not the refined self-interest view; this virtuous benevolence is not connected to how the person perceives herself, which is the first factor in the self-interest view.

Cases in which people engage in self-deception for reasons other than their own benefit are common and interesting but to my knowledge, excluding Funkhouser's (2017, 2019) and my (Krstić, 2021) analyses, they have not received notable attention. Quite often, people deceive themselves in order to protect a noble idea, value, ideal, or completely ridiculous belief. Some conspiracy theories seem to be good examples: millions of people believe that Elvis is alive; he has been spotted everywhere from Graceland to Russia. Or say that I cause myself to believe that a politician really did not have a sexual relationship with his assistant or that a priest did not molest children. Many of these cases could be explained by the hypothesis that what explains why these people deceive themselves is protecting the politician's face or some value associated with the important role of a priest, a professor, or a president. The self-deceiver engages in self-deception in order to avoid a belief that would devalue the sanctity of the priesthood in such a terrible way. And not only important values, self-deceivers may protect ideologies, such as the one about the supremacy of the white race. In fact, multiple factors explain why some deceivers deceive, and the same should be assumed for self-deception. By finding excuses for Mellissa, Stu could be avoiding a confrontation that both of them would find painful; two factors explain why he engages in deception. I call this self-deception *polyvalent* (Krstić, 2021).

In pretty much all the examples discussed here, self-interest does not explain why the person engages in self-deception even if they somehow benefit from deceiving themselves: this benefit is a side-effect. What I mean is that just as the heart beats to cause the blood to circulate (the behaviour's 'result') rather than to allow us to measure our pulse, which is the behaviour's side-effect, some self-deceivers deceive themselves to help others or to harm themselves (result) rather than to reduce their anxiety. They may thereby also reduce their anxiety, of course, but then this is the behaviour's side-effect, not the relevant result from my condition 1 (i.e., the reason why we have deception). We simply cannot come up with a single hypothesis account of the origin of self-deception. Just as in other-deception, we need a case-by-case analysis, which explains my condition 1. And this thesis is the final piece in my analysis.

5 Concluding Remarks

The main appeal of the traditional approach to self-deception is that it sits nicely with the intentionalist analysis of interpersonal deception. However, it also generates an untenable account of self-deception: if intending to deceive is necessary for deception, you cannot deceive yourself. You can deceive your *future* self, but this is not the kind of self-deception we want to understand, and we may assume that a part of your mind deceives another part of your mind or you as the main agent, but this hypothesis is unfalsifiable and it captures other-deception rather than self-deception; the self does not deceive the same self. The main appeal of deflating or eliminating this intention is that the resulting analyses do not generate a paradoxical account of self-deception. However, this comes at a high price of divorcing self-deception from deception: you cannot deceive yourself by accident or by mistake. Finally, most of the received analyses cannot make sense of possible animal self-deception.

My functional view avoids all these concerns in one simple move and it manages to deliver a unified analysis of deception and self-deception. According to my proposal, the *conditio sine qua non* of any account of deception (human or biological) is that the function of the behaviour or trait that misleads is to mislead. An agent can engage in deception and self-deception even if it does not intend to mislead as long as this condition is satisfied. Nevertheless, the view is consistent with the idea that some people deceive themselves intentionally. Our preferred analysis of self-deception should thus be functional. The mark of self-deception is not some reasoning discrepancy with her impartial cognitive peers but rather the person's 'not being herself'. Self-deceivers may end up with epistemically justified truth-directed mental states but they always violate their own norms of rationality; just like other-deceivers, they must 'not be themselves'. And, if they notice that they are not being their real selves, self-deceivers may exhibit some dissonance, discomfort, or behavioural tension. However, this tension is not a sign of a conceptually problematic irrationality or that they 'deep down' know the truth. It is just that the person suspects that something is off.

Cases of non-welcome, altruistic, benevolent, self-punishing, polyvalent, ideology- or value-driven self-deception are all evidence that self-deception need not be adaptive and that we cannot come up with a single hypothesis that explains why organisms engage in self-deception. True, in the majority of cases, self-deception is a defensive strategy, but even then, it need not be a self-defensive strategy: one might be defending someone else or an ideal rather than oneself. Because it allows a case-by-case analysis of why people engage in self-deception, the functional view can explain all possible cases of self-deception without any need for additional theoretical apparatus.

All in all, the functional analysis easily explains not only all instances of interpersonal deception and self-deception but also why some cases of self-deception are not adaptive or even maladaptive, and it provides a unified account of biological and human deception, including human and animal self-deception. No other theory can match that.

References

Angilletta, M. J. Kubitz, G., and Wilson, R. S. (2019). Self-Deception in Nonhuman Animals: Weak Crayfish Escalated Aggression as if They Were Strong. *Behavioral Ecology*, 30, 1469–1476. https://doi.org/10.1093/beheco/arz103.

Artiga, M. and Paternotte, C. (2018). Deception: A Functional Account. *Philosophical Studies*, 175, 579–600. https://doi.org/10.1007/s11098-017-0883-8.

(2024). Deception as Mimicry. *Philosophy of Science*, (Online First), 91 (2): 370–389. https://doi.org/10.1017/psa.2023.156.

Artiga, M., Schulte, P., and Fresco, N. Forthcoming. Some Proper Functions Are Distal. *British Journal for the Philosophy of Science*. https://doi.org/10.1086/735548.

Arvan, M. (2015). Job-Market Boot Camp, Part 16: The APA Interview. *The Philosophers' Cocoon*, https://philosopherscocoon.typepad.com/blog/2015/07/job-market-boot-camp-part-16-the-apa-interview.html.

Audi, R. (1982). Self-Deception, Action, and Will. *Erkenntnis*, 18, 133–158. https://doi.org/10.1007/bf00227930.

(1997). Self-Deception vs. Self-Caused Deception: A Comment on Professor Mele. *Behavioral and Brain Sciences*, 20, 104. https://doi.org/10.1017/S0140525X97230037.

Austin, J. L. (1956). A Plea for Excuses: The Presidential Address. *Proceedings of the Aristotelian Society*, 57, 1–30. https://doi.org/10.1093/aristotelian/57.1.1.

Bach, K. (1981). An Analysis of Self-Deception. *Philosophy and Phenomenological Research*, 41, 351–370. https://doi.org/10.2307/2107457.

(2009). Self-Deception. In A. Beckermann, B. P. McLaughlin, and S. Walter, eds., *The Oxford Handbook of Philosophy of Mind*. Oxford: Oxford University Press, pp. 781–796. https://doi.org/10.1093/oxfordhb/9780199262618.003.0046.

Barnes, A. (1997). *Seeing through Self-Deception*. New York: Cambridge University Press.

Bendaña, J. and Mandelbaum, E. (2021). The Fragmentation of Belief. In C. Borgoni, D. Kindermann, and A. Onofri, eds., *The Fragmentation of Belief*. Oxford: Oxford University Press, pp. 78–107. https://doi.org/10.1093/oso/9780198850670.003.0004.

Bentall, R. P. (1994). Cognitive Biases and Abnormal Beliefs: Towards a Model of Persecutory Delusions. In A. S. David and J. C. Cutting, eds., *The Neuropsychology of Schizophrenia*. Hove: Psychology Press, pp. 337–360.

Bermúdez, J. L. (2000). Self-Deception, Intentions, and Contradictory Beliefs. *Analysis*, 60, 309–319. https://doi.org/10.1111/1467-8284.00247.

Birch, J. (2014). Propositional Content in Signaling Systems. *Philosophical Studies*, 171, 493–512. https://doi.org/10.1007/s11098-014-0280-5.

  (2019). Altruistic Deception. *Studies in History and Philosophy of Science Part C: Studies in History and Philosophy of Biological and Biomedical Sciences*, 74, 27–33. https://doi.org/10.1016/j.shpsc.2019.01.004.

Borgoni, C., Kindermann D., and Onofri, A. eds. (2021). *The Fragmentation of Belief*. Oxford: Oxford University Press.

Carlini, E. A. and Maia, L. O. (2017). Plant and Fungal Hallucinogens as Toxic and Therapeutic Agents. In P. Gopalakrishnakone, C. R. Carlini, and R. Ligabue-Braun, eds., *Plant Toxins*. Dordrecht: Springer Netherlands, pp. 37–80. https://doi.org/10.1007/978-94-007-6464-4_6.

Carson, T. L. (2010). *Lying and Deception: Theory and Practice*. Oxford: Oxford University Press.

Chan, C. Y. and Rowbottom, D. P. (2019). Self-Deception and Shifting Degrees of Belief. *Philosophical Psychology*, 32, 1204–1220. https://doi.org/10.1080/09515089.2019.1646419.

Curzer, H. J. (2024a). Akratic and Beneficial Intentional Self-Deception. *Inquiry*, (Online First), 1–28. https://doi.org/10.1080/0020174X.2024.2420354.

  (2024b). Self-Deception and Dissociation. *Erkenntnis*, (Online First), 1–20. https://doi.org/10.1007/s10670-024-00888-3.

Davidson, D. (1963). Actions, Reasons, and Causes. *The Journal of Philosophy*, 60, 685–700. https://doi.org/10.2307/2023177.

  (1985). Incoherence and Irrationality. *Dialectica*, 39, 345–354. https://doi.org/10.1111/j.1746-8361.1985.tb01603.x.

  (1986). Deception and Division. In his *Problems of Rationality*. Oxford: Oxford University Press, pp. 199–212. https://doi.org/10.1093/0198237545.003.0013.

  (1997). Who Is Fooled. In his *Problems of Rationality*. Oxford: Oxford University Press, pp. 213–230. https://doi.org/10.1093/0198237545.003.0014.

DePaulo, B. M., Kashy, D. A., Kirkendol, S., Wyer, M., and Epstein, J. A. (1996). Lying in Everyday Life. *Journal of Personality and Social Psychology*, 70, 979–995. https://doi.org/10.1037/0022-3514.70.5.979.

DePaulo, B. M. (2019). Lying in Social Psychology. In J. Meibauer, ed., *The Oxford Handbook of Lying*. Oxford: Oxford University Press, pp. 436–445.

Derksen, A. A. (2001). The Seven Strategies of the Sophisticated Pseudo-Scientist: A Look into Freud's Rhetorical Tool Box. *Journal for General Philosophy of Science*, 32, 329–350. https://doi.org/10.1023/A:1013100717113.

Deweese-Boyd, I. (2021). Self-Deception. In E. N. Zalta, ed., *The Stanford Encyclopedia of Philosophy*. https://plato.stanford.edu/archives/sum2021/entries/self-deception/.

Dietz, S. (2019). White and Prosocial Lies. In J. Meibauer, ed., *The Oxford Handbook of Lying*. Oxford: Oxford University Press, pp. 287–299.

Dolcini, N. (2016). The Pragmatics of Self-Deception. In L. Felline, A. Ledda, F. Paoli, and E. Rossanese, eds., *New Directions in Logic and the Philosophy of Science*. Cambridge: College, pp. 67–76.

Doody, P. (2017). Is There Evidence of Robust, Unconscious Self Deception? A Reply to Funkhouser and Barrett. *Philosophical Psychology*, 30, 657–676. https://doi.org/10.1080/09515089.2017.1328491.

Egan, A. (2008). Seeing and Believing: Perception, Belief Formation and the Divided Mind. *Philosophical Studies*, 140, 47–63. https://doi.org/10.1007/s11098-008-9225-1.

  (2009). Imagination, Delusion, and Self-Deception. In T. Bayne and J. Fernández, eds., *Delusion and Self-Deception: Motivational and Affective Influences on Belief-Formation*. New York: Psychology Press, pp. 263–280.

Epley, N. and Whitchurch, E. (2008). Mirror, Mirror on the Wall: Enhancement in Self Recognition. *Personality and Social Psychology Bulletin*, 34, 1159–1170. https://doi.org/10.1177/0146167208318601.

Erat, S. and Gneezy, U. (2012). White Lies. *Management Science*, 58, 732–773. https://doi.org/10.1287/mnsc.1110.1449.

Fagerberg, H. and Garson, J. (2024). Proper Functions Are Proximal Functions. *British Journal for the Philosophy of Science*. https://doi.org/10.1086/731869.

Fallis, D. (2015a). What Is Disinformation? *Library Trends*, 63, 401–426. https://doi.org/10.1353/lib.2015.0014.

  (2015b). Skyrms on the Possibility of Universal Deception. *Philosophical Studies*, 172, 375–397. https://doi.org/10.1007/s11098-014-0308-x.

Fallis, D. and Lewis, P. J. (2019). Toward a Formal Analysis of Deceptive Signalling. *Synthese*, 196, 2279–2303. https://doi.org/10.1007/s11229-017-1536-3.

  (2021). Animal Deception and the Content of Signals. *Studies in History and Philosophy of Science Part A*, 87, 114–124. https://doi.org/10.1016/j.shpsa.2021.03.004.

Faulkner, P. (2013). Lying and Deceit. In H. LaFollette, ed., *The International Encyclopedia of Ethics*. Oxford: Wiley-Blackwell, pp. 3101–3109.

Fernández, J. (2013). Self-Deception and Self-Knowledge. *Philosophical Studies*, 162, 379–400. https://doi.org/10.1007/s11098-011-9771-9.

Fingarette, H. (1998). Self-Deception Needs No Explaining. *The Philosophical Quarterly*, 48, 289–301. https://doi.org/10.1111/1467-9213.00101.

Friedrich, J. (1993). Primary Error Detection and Minimization PEDMIN Strategies in Social Cognition: A Reinterpretation of Confirmation Bias Phenomena. *Psychological Review*, 100, 298–319. https://doi.org/10.1037/0033-295x.100.2.298.

Funkhouser, E. (2005). Do the Self-Deceived Get What They Want? *Pacific Philosophical Quarterly*, 86, 295–312. https://doi.org/10.1111/j.1468-0114.2005.00228.x.

(2009). Self-Deception and the Limits of Folk Psychology. *Social Theory and Practice*, 35, 1–13. https://doi.org/10.5840/soctheorpract20093511.

(2017). Is Self-Deception an Effective Non-cooperative Strategy? *Biology and Philosophy*, 32, 221–242. https://doi.org/10.1007/s10539-016-9550-2.

(2019). *Self-Deception*. London: Routledge.

Funkhouser, E. and Barrett, D. (2016). Robust, Unconscious Self-Deception: Strategic and Flexible. *Philosophical Psychology*, 29, 682–696. http://dx.doi.org/10.1080/09515089.2015.1134769.

Funkhouser, E. and Hallam, K. (2024). Self-Handicapping and Self-Deception: A Two-Way Street. *Philosophical Psychology*, 37, 299–324. https://doi.org/10.1080/09515089.2022.2055915.

Gadsby, S. (2022). Imposter Syndrome and Self-Deception. *Australasian Journal of Philosophy*, 100, 247–261. https://doi.org/10.1080/00048402.2021.1874445.

Galeotti, A. E. (2012). Self-Deception: Intentional Plan or Mental Event? *Humana.Mente: Journal of Philosophical Studies*, 20, 41–66.

(2018). *Political Self-Deception*. Cambridge: Cambridge University Press.

Garson, J. (2019). *What Biological Functions Are and Why They Matter*. Cambridge: Cambridge University Press.

Gendler, T. S. (2007). Self-Deception as Pretense. *Philosophical Perspectives*, 21, 231–258. https://doi.org/10.1111/j.1520-8583.2007.00127.x.

Gerrans, P. (2014). *The Measure of Madness: Philosophy of Mind, Cognitive Neuroscience, and Delusional Thought*. Cambridge, MA: The MIT Press.

Gneezy, U. (2005). Deception: The Role of Consequences. *American Economic Review*, 95, 384–394. https://doi.org/10.1257/0002828053828662.

Grossmann, T. (2023). The Human Fear Paradox: Affective Origins of Cooperative Care. *Behavioral and Brain Sciences*, 46, E52. https://doi.org/10.1017/S0140525X2200067X.

References

Gur, R. C. and Sackeim, H. A. (1979). Self-Deception: A Concept in Search of a Phenomenon. *Journal of Personality and Social Psychology*, 37, 147–169. https://psycnet.apa.org/doi/10.1037/0022-3514.37.2.147.

Guthrie, R. D. and Petocz, R. G. (1970). Weapon Automimicry among Animals. *The American Naturalist*, 104, 585–588. https://doi.org/10.1086/282694.

Holton, R. (2001). What Is the Role of Self in Self-deception. *Proceedings of the Aristotelian Society*, 101, 53–69. https://doi.org/10.1111/j.0066-7372.2003.00021.x.

John, O. P. and Robins, R. W. (1994). Accuracy and Bias in Self-Perception: Individual Differences in Self-Enhancement and Narcissism. *Journal of Personality and Social Psychology*, 66, 206–219. https://psycnet.apa.org/doi/10.1037/0022-3514.66.1.206.

Johnston, M. (1988). Self-Deception and the Nature of Mind. In B. McLaughlin and A. Rorty, eds., *Perspectives on Self-Deception*. Berkeley: University of California Press, pp. 63–91.

Jordan, M. (2019). Secondary Self-Deception. *Ratio*, 32, 122–130. https://doi.org/10.1111/rati.12235.

  (2020). Literal Self-Deception. *Analysis*, 80, 248–256. https://doi.org/10.1093/analys/anz053.

Kelsky, K. (2012). The 'Be Yourself' Myth: Performing the Academic Self on the Job Market. http://theprofessorisin.com/2012/03/20/the-be-yourself-myth-performing-the-academic-self-on-the-job-market/.

Kenny, D. A. and Kashy, D. A. (1994). Enhanced Co-orientation in the Perception of Friends: A Social Relations Analysis. *Journal of Personality and Social Psychology*, 67, 1024–1033. https://doi.org/10.1037/0022-3514.67.6.1024.

Korczyk, K. (2024). Absorbed in Deceit: Modeling Intention-Driven Self-Deception with Agential Layering. *Inquiry* (Online First), 1–27. https://doi.org/10.1080/0020174X.2024.2406891.

Krstić, V. (2020a). Transparent Delusion. *Review of Philosophy and Psychology*, 11, 183–201. https://doi.org/10.1007/s13164-019-00457-6.

  (2020b). On the Nature of Indifferent Lies, a Reply to Rutschmann and Wiegmann. *Philosophical Psychology*, 33, 757–771. https://doi.org/10.1080/09515089.2020.1743255.

  (2021). On the Function of Self-Deception. *The European Journal of Philosophy*, 29, 846–863. https://doi.org/10.1111/ejop.12608.

  (2023a). Lying to Others, Lying to Yourself, and Literal Self-Deception. *Inquiry*, (Online First), 1–26. https://doi.org/10.1080/0020174X.2023.2206850.

  (2023b). Lying: Revisiting the Intending to Deceive Condition. *Analysis*, 83, 249–259. https://doi.org/10.1093/analys/anac099.

(2023c). Fearful Apes or Nervous Goats? Another Look at Functions of Dispositions or Traits. *Behavioral and Brain Sciences*, 46, E68.

(2023d). Lying by Asserting What You Believe to Be True: A Case of Transparent Delusion. *Review of Philosophy and Psychology*, 15, 1423–1443. https://osf.io/v73un.

(2024b). Manipulation, Deception, the Victim's Reasoning, and Her Evidence. *Analysis*, 84, 267–275. https://doi.org/10.1093/analys/anad064.

(2024c). A Functional Analysis of Human Deception. *Journal of American Philosophical Association*, 10, 836–854. https://doi.org/10.10 17/apa.2023.19.

(2025). We Should Move on from Signalling-Based Analyses of Biological Deception. *Erkenntnis*, 90, 545–565. https://doi.org/10.1007/s10670-023-00719-x (Forthcoming). A Functional Analysis of Self-Deception. *Journal of American Philosophical Association*.

Krstić, V. and Saville, C. (2019). Deception (Under Uncertainty) as a Kind of Manipulation. *Australasian Journal of Philosophy*, 97, 830–835. https://doi.org/10.1080/00048402.2019.1604777.

Langer, E. J. and Rodin, J. (1976). The Effects of Choice and Enhanced Personal Responsibility for the Aged: A Field Experiment in an Institutional Setting. *Journal of Personality and Social Psychology*, 34, 191–198. https://doi.org/10.1037//0022-3514.34.2.191.

Lauria, F., Preissmann, D., and Clément, F. (2016). Self-Deception as Affective Coping: An Empirical Perspective on Philosophical Issues. *Consciousness and Cognition*, 41, 119–134. https://doi.org/10.1016/j.concog.2016.02.001.

Lazar, A. (1999). Deceiving Oneself or Self-Deceived? On the Formation of Beliefs 'Under the Influence'. *Mind*, 108, 263–290. https://doi.org/10.1093/mind/108.430.265.

Lev-Yadun, S. (2003). Weapon (thorn) Automimicry and Mimicry of Aposematic Colorful Thorns in Plants. *Journal of Theoretical Biology*, 224, 183–188.

Levy, N. (2004). Self-Deception and Moral Responsibility. *Ratio*, 17, 294–311. https://doi.org/10.1111/j.0034-0006.2004.00255.x.

(2016). Have I Turned the Stove Off? Explaining Everyday Anxiety. *Philosophers' Imprint*, 16, 1–10. http://hdl.handle.net/2027/spo.3521354.0016.002.

Lick, D. J., Cortland, C. I., and Johnson, K. L. (2016). The Pupils Are the Windows to Sexuality: Pupil Dilation as a Visual Cue to Others' Sexual Interest. *Evolution and Human Behavior*, 37, 117–124. https://doi.org/10.1016/j.evolhumbehav.2015.09.004.

Linsky, L. (1963). Deception. *Inquiry*, 6, 157–169. https://doi.org/10.1080/00201746308601371.

Livingstone Smith, D. (2014). Self-Deception: A Teleofunctional Approach. *Philosophia*, 42, 181–199. https://doi.org/10.1007/s11406-013-9464-z.

Lockie, R. (2003). Depth Psychology and Self-Deception. *Philosophical Psychology*, 16, 127–148. https://doi.org/10.1080/0951508032000067707.

Lynch, K. (2012). On the 'Tension' Inherent in Self-Deception. *Philosophical Psychology*, 25, 433–450. https://doi.org/10.1080/09515089.2011.622364.

(2016). Willful Ignorance and Self-Deception. *Philosophical Studies*, 173, 505–523. https://doi.org/10.1007/s11098-015-0504-3.

(2017). An Agentive Non-intentionalist Theory of Self-Deception. *Canadian Journal of Philosophy*, 47, 779–798. https://doi.org/10.1080/00455091.2017.1321909.

Mahon, J. E. (2007). A Definition of Deceiving. *International Journal of Applied Philosophy*, 21, 181–194. https://doi.org/10.5840/ijap20072124.

(2016). The Definition of Lying and Deception. In E. N. Zalta, ed., *The Stanford Encyclopedia of Philosophy*. https://plato.stanford.edu/archives/win2016/entries/lying-definition/.

Marcus, E. (2019). Reconciling Practical Knowledge with Self-Deception. *Mind*, 128, 1205–1225. https://doi.org/10.1093/mind/fzy061.

McKay, R. T. and Dennett, D. C. (2009). The Evolution of Misbelief. *Behavioral and Brain Sciences*, 32, 493–451. https://doi.org/10.1017/s0140525x09990975.

McWhirter, G. (2016). Behavioural Deception and Formal Models of Communication. *British Journal for the Philosophy of Science*, 67, 757–780. https://doi.org/10.1093/bjps/axv001.

Mele, A. R. (1987). *Irrationality – An Essay on Akrasia, Self-deception, and Self-control*. Oxford: Oxford University Press

(1997). Real Self-Deception. *Behavioral and Brain Sciences*, 20, 91–136. https://doi.org/10.1017/S0140525X97000034.

(1999). Twisted Self-deception. *Philosophical Psychology*, 12, 117–137.

(2001). *Self-Deception Unmasked*. Princeton: Princeton University Press.

(2006). Self-deception and Delusions. *European Journal of Analytic Philosophy*, 2, 109–124.

(2009). Delusional Confabulations and Self-Deception. In W. Hirstein, ed., *Confabulation: Views from Neuroscience, Psychiatry, Psychology and Philosophy*. Oxford: Oxford University Press, pp. 139–158. https://doi.org/10.1093/acprof:oso/9780199208913.003.06.

(2010). Approaching Self-Deception: How Robert Audi and I Part Company. *Consciousness and Cognition*, 19, 745–750. https://doi.org/10.1016/j.concog.2010.06.009.

(2020). Self-Deception and Selectivity. *Philosophical Studies*, 177, 2697–2711. https://doi.org/10.1007/s11098-019-01334-9.

Michel, C. and Newen, A. (2010). Self-Deception as Pseudo-rational Regulation of Belief. *Consciousness and Cognition*, 19, 731–744. https://doi.org/10.1016/j.concog.2010.06.019.

Mijović-Prelec, D. and Prelec, D. (2010). Self-Deception as Self-Signalling: A Model and Experimental Evidence. *Philosophical Transactions: Biological Sciences*, 365, 227–240. https://doi.org/10.1098/rstb.2009.0218.

Nelkin, D. (2002). Self-Deception, Motivation and the Desire to Believe. *Pacific Philosophical Quarterly*, 83, 384–406. https://doi.org/10.1111/1468-0114.t01-1-00156.

Passos, I. D. and Mironidou-Tzouveleki, M. (2016). Hallucinogenic Plants in the Mediterranean Countries. In V. R. Preedy, ed., *Neuropathology of Drug Addictions and Substance Misuse; Volume 2: Stimulants, Club and Dissociative Drugs, Hallucinogens, Steroids, Inhalants and International Aspects*. London: Academic Press, pp. 761–772. https://doi.org/10.1016/B978-0-12-800212-4.00071-6.

Pataki, T. (1997). Self-Deception and Wish-Fulfilment. *Philosophia*, 25, 297–322. https://doi.org/10.1007/BF02380036.

Patten, D. (2003). How Do We Deceive Ourselves? *Philosophical Psychology*, 16, 229–246. https://doi.org/10.1080/09515080307767.

Pears, D. (1982). Motivated Irrationality, Freudian Theory and Cognitive Dissonance. In R. Wollheim, ed., *Philosophical Essays on Freud*. Cambridge: Cambridge University Press, pp. 264–288. https://doi.org/10.1017/CBO9780511554636.017.

(1986). The Goals and Strategies of Self-Deception. In J. Elster, ed., *The Multiple Self*. Cambridge: Cambridge University Press, pp. 59–78.

(1991). Self-Deceptive Belief-Formation. *Synthese*, 89, 393–405. https://doi.org/10.1007/BF00413504.

Quattrone, G. A. and Tversky, A. (1984). Causal versus Diagnostic Contingencies: On Self-Deception and on the Voter's Illusion. *Journal of Personality and Social Psychology*, 46, 237–248. https://psycnet.apa.org/doi/10.1037/0022-3514.46.2.237.

Quilty-Dunn, J. and Mandelbaum, E. (2018). Against Dispositionalism: Belief in Cognitive Science. *Philosophical Studies*, 175, 2353–2372. https://doi.org/10.1007/s11098-017-0962-x.

Rieger, G. and Savin-Williams, R. C. (2012). The Eyes Have It: Sex and Sexual Orientation Differences in Pupil Dilation Patterns. *PLoS One*, 7, e40256. https://doi.org/10.1371/journal.pone.0040256.

Saul, J. M. (2013). *Lying, Misleading, and What Is Said: An Exploration in Philosophy of Language and in Ethics*. Oxford: Oxford University Press.

Scott-Kakures, D. (1996). Self-Deception and Internal Irrationality. *Philosophy and Phenomenological Research*, 56, 31–56. https://doi.org/10.2307/2108464.

(2000). Motivated Believing: Wishful and Unwelcome. *Noûs*, 34, 348–375. https://doi.org/10.1111/0029-4624.00215.

(2001). High Anxiety: Barnes on What Moves the Unwelcome Believer. *Philosophical Psychology*, 14, 313–326. https://doi.org/10.1080/09515080120072622.

(2002). At 'Permanent Risk': Reasoning and Self-Knowledge in Self-Deception. *Philosophy and Phenomenological Research*, 65, 576–603. https://doi.org/10.1111/j.1933-1592.2002.tb00222.x.

(2009). Unsettling Questions: Cognitive Dissonance in Self-Deception. *Social Theory and Practice*, 35, 73–106. https://doi.org/10.5840/soctheorpract20093515.

(2021). Self-Deceptive Inquiry: Disorientation, Doubt, Dissonance. *Midwest Studies in Philosophy*, 45, 457–482. https://doi.org/10.5840/msp2021101213.

Searcy, W. A. and Nowicki, S. (2005). *The Evolution of Animal Communication: Reliability and Deception in Signaling Systems*. Princeton: Princeton University Press.

Šekrst, K. (2022). Everybody Lies: Deception Levels in Various Domains of Life. *Biosemiotics*, (Online First), 15, 309–324. https://doi.org/10.1007/s12304-022-09485-9.

Sharpsteen, D. J. and Kirkpatrick, L. A. (1997). Romantic Jealousy and Adult Romantic Attachment. *Journal of Personality and Social Psychology*, 72, 627–640. https://doi.org/10.1037/0022-3514.72.3.627.

Shea, N., Godfrey-Smith, P., and Cao, R. (2018). Content in Simple Signalling Systems. *British Journal for the Philosophy of Science*, 69, 1009–1035. https://doi.org/10.1093/bjps/axw036.

Skyrms, B. (2010). *Signals*. New York: Oxford University Press.

Skyrms, B. and Barrett, J. A. (2019). Propositional Content in Signals. *Studies in History and Philosophy of Science Part C: Studies in History and Philosophy of Biological and Biomedical Sciences*, 74, 34–39. https://doi.org/10.1016/j.shpsc.2019.01.005.

Snyder, C. R., Irving, L. M., Sigmon, S. T., and Holleran, S. (1992). Reality Negotiation and Valence/Linkage of Self-Theories: Psychic Showdown at the 'I'm OK' Corral and Beyond. In L. Montada, S.-H. Filipp, and

M. J. Lerner, eds., *Life Crises and Experience of Loss in Adulthood*. Hillsdale: Erlbaum, pp. 275–297.

Sorensen, R. (1984). Self-Deception and Scattered Events. *Mind*, 94, 64–69. https://doi.org/10.1093/mind/XCIV.373.64.

Swann, W. B. Jr. (1983). Self-Verification: Bringing Social Reality into Harmony with the Self. In J. Suls and A. G. Greenwald, eds., *Social Psychological Perspectives on the Self, Vol. 2*. New York: Erlbaum, pp. 33–66.

Szabados, B. (1974). Self-Deception. *Canadian Journal of Philosophy*, 4, 51–68. https://doi.org/10.2307/2219163.

Taylor, C. R. L., Skokan, L. A., and Aspinwall, L. G. (1989). Maintaining Positive Illusions in the Face of Negative Information: Getting the Facts without Letting Them Get to You. *Journal of Social and Clinical Psychology*, 8, 114–129. https://psycnet.apa.org/doi/10.1521/jscp.1989.8.2.114.

Taylor, M., Martin, B., and Wilsdon, J. (2010). The Scientific Century: Securing our Future Prosperity. *The Royal Society*, The Scientific Century: Securing Our Future Prosperity (royalsociety.org)

Taylor, S. E. and Brown, J. D. (1988). Illusion and Well-Being: A Social Psychological Perspective on Mental Health. *Psychological Bulletin*, 103, 193–210. https://psycnet.apa.org/doi/10.1037/0033-2909.103.2.193.

Tombs, S. and Silverman, I. (2004). Pupillometry; A Sexual Selection Approach. *Evolution and Human Behavior*, 25, 221–228. https://doi.org/10.1016/j.evolhumbehav.2004.05.001.

Trivers, R. (2011). *The Folly of Fools; the Logic of Deceit and Self-Deception in Human Life*. New York: Basic Books.

Trope, Y. and Liberman, A. (1996). Social Hypothesis Testing: Cognitive and Motivational Mechanisms. In E. Higgins and E. Kruglanski, eds., *Social Psychology: A Handbook of Basic Principles*. New York: Guilford Press, pp. 239–270.

Van Horne, W. A. (1981). Prolegomenon to a Theory of Deception. *Philosophy and Phenomenological Research*, 42, 171–182. https://doi.org/10.2307/2107289.

Van Leeuwen, N. (2007a). The Product of Self-Deception. *Erkenntnis*, 67, 419–437. https://doi.org/10.1007/s10670-007-9058-x.

(2007b). The Spandrels of Self-Deception: Prospects for a Biological Theory of a Mental Phenomenon. *Philosophical Psychology*, 20, 329–348. https://psycnet.apa.org/doi/10.1080/09515080701197148.

(2009). Self-Deception Won't Make You Happy. *Social Theory and Practice*, 35, 107–132. https://doi.org/10.5840/soctheorpract20093516.

Von Hippel, W. and Trivers, R. (2011). The Evolution and Psychology of Self-Deception. *Behavioral and Brain Sciences*, 34, 1–16. https://doi.org/10.1017/S0140525X10001354.

Wehofsits, A. (2023). The Relationship between Self-Deception and Other-Deception. *The Southern Journal of Philosophy*, 62, 263–275. https://doi.org/10.1111/sjp.12540.

West-Eberhard, M. J. (1979). Sexual Selection, Social Competition, and Evolutions. *Proceedings of The American Philosophical Society*, 123, 222–234. https://doi.org/10.1086/413215.

Acknowledgements

I thank the three anonymous reviewers for their helpful and constructive comments. I also thank everyone who has ever commented on my work in good faith.

Some material in this book is reworked from some of my recently published articles, 'On the Function of Self-Deception', 'A Functional Analysis of Human Deception', and 'A Functional Analysis of Self-Deception'. In the meantime, some of my views have changed.

To Silly Slatky Girl

Cambridge Elements ≡

Epistemology

Stephen Hetherington
University of New South Wales, Sydney

Stephen Hetherington is Professor Emeritus of Philosophy at the University of New South Wales, Sydney. He is the author of numerous books, including *Knowledge and the Gettier Problem* (Cambridge University Press, 2016), and *What Is Epistemology?* (Polity, 2019), and is the editor of several others, including *Knowledge in Contemporary Epistemology* (with Markos Valaris: Bloomsbury, 2019), and *What the Ancients Offer to Contemporary Epistemology* (with Nicholas D. Smith: Routledge, 2020). He was the Editor-in-Chief of the Australasian Journal of Philosophy from 2013 until 2022.

About the Series

This Elements series seeks to cover all aspects of a rapidly evolving field, including emerging and evolving topics such as: fallibilism; knowing how; self-knowledge; knowledge of morality; knowledge and injustice; formal epistemology; knowledge and religion; scientific knowledge; collective epistemology; applied epistemology; virtue epistemology; wisdom. The series demonstrates the liveliness and diversity of the field, while also pointing to new areas of investigation.

Cambridge Elements

Epistemology

Elements in the Series

The Nature and Normativity of Defeat
Christoph Kelp

Philosophy, Bullshit, and Peer Review
Neil Levy

Stratified Virtue Epistemology: A Defence
J. Adam Carter

The Skeptic and the Veridicalist: On the Difference Between Knowing What There Is and Knowing What Things Are
Yuval Avnur

Transcendental Epistemology
Tony Cheng

Knowledge and God
Matthew A. Benton

Knowing What It Is Like
Yuri Cath

Disagreement
Diego E. Machuca

On Believing and Being Convinced
Paul Silva Jr

Knowledge-First Epistemology: A Defence
Mona Simion

Emotional Self-Knowledge: How Affective Skills Reveal Our Values, Goals, Cares and Concerns
Matt Stichter and Ellen Fridland

Deception and Self-Deception: A Unified Account
Vladimir Krstić

A full series listing is available at: www.cambridge.org/EEPI

Printed by Libri Plureos GmbH in Hamburg, Germany